Coconut Every Day

Coconut Every Day
Cooking with Nature's Miracle Superfood

SASHA SEYMOUR

Photography by Kathleen Finlay

PINTAIL

PINTAIL
a member of Penguin Group (USA)

PUBLISHED BY THE PENGUIN GROUP
Penguin Canada Books Inc., 90 Eglinton Avenue East, Suite 700,
Toronto, Ontario, Canada M4P 2Y3

PENGUIN GROUP (USA) LLC, 375 Hudson Street, New York, New York 10014, U.S.A.
PENGUIN BOOKS LTD, 80 Strand, London WC2R 0RL, England
PENGUIN IRELAND, 25 St Stephen's Green, Dublin 2, Ireland (a division of Penguin Books Ltd)
PENGUIN GROUP (AUSTRALIA), 707 Collins Street, Melbourne, Victoria 3008,
    Australia (a division of Pearson Australia Group Pty Ltd)
PENGUIN BOOKS INDIA PVT LTD, 11 Community Centre, Panchsheel Park,
    New Delhi – 110 017, India
PENGUIN GROUP (NZ), 67 Apollo Drive, Rosedale, Auckland 0632, New Zealand
    (a division of Pearson New Zealand Ltd)
PENGUIN BOOKS (SOUTH AFRICA) (PTY) LTD, 24 Sturdee Avenue, Rosebank,
    Johannesburg 2196, South Africa

PENGUIN BOOKS LTD, REGISTERED OFFICES: 80 Strand, London WC2R 0RL, England

Published in Penguin paperback by Penguin Canada Books Inc., 2014
Published in this edition, 2014

1 2 3 4 5 6 7 8 9 10 (CR)

Copyright © Sasha Seymour, 2014

Food and prop styling by Sasha Seymour
Photography by Kathleen Finlay
Photo on page 156 by John Cullen

Manufactured in the U.S.A.

ISBN: 978-0-14-319074-5

Visit the Penguin US website at **www.penguin.com**

CONTENTS

Foreword

BY JOY McCARTHY

As a nutritionist, I consider coconut products—especially coconut oil—to be essential in my kitchen. I've written extensively about it on my blog, Joyous Health, and tell pretty much anyone and everyone who'll listen how much I love coconut products and how coconut can benefit them from a health perspective. It is truly a superfood.

After reviewing these drool-worthy recipes that Sasha has created (and letting my husband know that we must make the Banana Coconut Ricotta Pancakes for our next Sunday brunch), I was reminded on this beautiful journey of coconut of the varied and delicious uses of coconut products, including milk, flour, flakes, sugar, and water.

Apparently I'm not the only lover of coconut products. In fact, the coconut has been valued for thousands of years, and rightly so! Scriptures of Hinduism dating back to 1500 B.C.E. say it nourishes the body, increases strength, and promotes beautiful hair and skin. In Ayurveda medicine, it has been used for over 4000 years as an effective treatment for skin diseases.

In the Philippines, the coconut plant is called the "tree of life." Interestingly, a country where coconut oil appears in virtually every single dish also has the lowest cancer rates of the 50 countries surveyed by the National Cancer Institute.

The health benefits of coconut are as plentiful as the many ways to eat it.

PROMOTES WEIGHT LOSS

Studies have shown that when coconut oil is part of one's diet, white fat stores are reduced. Because of the medium-chain triglycerides (MCTs) being so well absorbed and used as an energy source, their burning actually increases metabolic rate.

A study showed that over a six-day period a diet high in MCTs increased thermogenesis by a whopping 50 percent—talk about fat-burning potential just by adding coconut oil or milk to your smoothie! I know what I'll be making tomorrow: the Brain Power Smoothie (page 40).

SAFEST OIL FOR COOKING

Because it's a saturated fat, coconut oil is very stable and can withstand high heat without smoking, making it ideal for cooking, sautéing, and roasting food. Plus it tastes absolutely deeeelish!

BRAIN FOOD

Insulin problems, which millions of North Americans suffer from, prevent brain cells from accepting glucose, the primary source of energy for your brain. Without glucose, cells eventually die. However, the brain readily accepts ketones as a source of fuel. There's now evidence suggesting that ketone bodies may actually help restore and renew neurons and nerve function in your brain, even after damage has set in. Ketones are metabolized in the liver after digesting coconut oil because it's such a wonderful source of MCTs. Additionally, coconut oil has been making waves in the media for its link to the prevention of Alzheimer's disease. Because of this, Florida researchers are currently studying the effects of coconut oil in the prevention of Alzheimer's disease. This is very exciting news for the treatment of a disease that affects millions of people.

EXTREMELY HIGH IN FIBER

Coconut flour is one of my favorite flours to bake with, as it has the highest amount of fiber of all flours. This makes it blood-sugar-balancing, which means you can say bye-bye to those pesky afternoon cravings. How does it do this? Fiber slows the release of glucose into the bloodstream. When glucose levels are balanced, insulin levels are kept in check, which aids in managing cravings.

A WONDERFUL DAIRY ALTERNATIVE

Not only do coconut products have numerous health benefits, but as you'll see in Sasha's recipes, they're also the perfect substitute when cooking for those with dairy allergies and sensitivities. You can now eat cream sauces without a bellyache, thanks to Sasha's Soft Scrambled Eggs with Creamed Spinach and Smoked Salmon and Cream of Wild Mushroom Soup—my mouth is watering just writing this!

GO GLUTEN-FREE

Gluten intolerance is hitting epidemic proportions, but you don't have to worry because coconut products are naturally gluten-free. Pumpkin Spice Muffins or Coconut Chicken Fingers without gluten?

IMMUNE-ENHANCING

As much as 50 percent of the fatty acids in coconut are in the form of medium-chain (12-carbon) saturated fat called "lauric acid." The only other abundant source of this healing fat is breast milk. Your body converts this to a highly beneficial compound called monolaurin, an antiviral/antibacterial that destroys a wide variety of disease-causing organisms. *H. Pylori*, yeast, fungi, protozoa, and a number of species of ringworm are all destroyed by lauric acid.

BEAUTIFYING NATURALLY

After trying these scrumptious recipes in *Coconut Every Day* you'll probably want to only eat coconut products, but when applied topically they're also beautifying. In fact, coconut oil is a fantastic deep-conditioning treatment for your hair, a nourishing lip moisturizer, and an alternative to shaving cream for your legs. But who wants to use it on their body when Sasha has provided so many flavorful ways to get it into our belly?

BREASTFEEDING MAMAS

A study from the *American Journal of Clinical Nutrition* found that lactating mothers who include virgin coconut oil in their diet have higher amounts of capric acid in their breast milk. Combined with coconut oil's other healthy fats, lauric and caprylic acid, there is an increase in high-density lipoproteins, otherwise known as HDL (many refer to it as "good cholesterol"). Why is this helpful? Children are better protected from infections and toxins. Interestingly, researchers at the University of California–Davis found that children with infections had high levels of LDL relative to HDL. Go coconut oil!

I'm really excited that this book has landed in your hands, because these superbly wonderful recipes featuring my favorite superfood, coconut, were created with love by Sasha and will certainly set you on a path to joyous health.

Joy McCarthy, CNP, RNCP, is the vibrant nutritionist behind the popular blog and bestselling book, *Joyous Health*

Introduction

Deep down in the mind of many a good cook, countless recipes lurk. For the most part, getting them out is just a matter of knowing where to start, finding a little inspiration, or being faced with a great ingredient and knowing what to do with it. I started with coconut.

I got a lot of surprised looks when I'd tell people I was writing a coconut book. Why on earth coconut? people would wonder. But trust me, coconut is on its way to being the next big thing. Our neighborhood grocery store started stocking coconut milk—well, that's been around forever—but then they started carrying coconut water, and then coconut oil, and coconut butter and coconut sugar. It's practically epidemic at this point! But when I starting looking for recipes that used all these things, I found that the one ingredient missing was a coconut cookbook.

Well, here it is. *Coconut Every Day* grew out of a seed planted by its publisher. She came to me and the photographer and said, "I have an exciting idea." And it *has* been exciting. A whirlwind of learning and cooking and having ideas and scrapping them. Of digging around in the cuisines of cultures that use coconut every day, literally. My household, and extensions of it, lived coconut every day, too.

The coconut is a miracle food. A saturated fat that gets burned like a carbohydrate? And that can increase your metabolism, and lower your cholesterol, *and* fight candida? Yes! And it tastes good, to boot.

I started off slowly, replacing dairy with coconut milk or coconut oil in some of my favorite recipes, and as I got going, I realized that we Western eaters have such a limited pantry. Every meal has either a wheat or a dairy component. Toast for breakfast, a bagel for lunch, and maybe pasta for dinner, and all of it usually covered in some kind of dairy product. How would we feel if we replaced some of those foods with a more nutritious alternative? Probably pretty darn good.

So here it is. The result of months of standing in the middle of the kitchen every morning thinking, What would I like to eat today? I'd go to the store and get inspired by all the good things available, then I'd start thinking about how to make the recipe in my head healthier. We don't have to stop eating the foods we love, but we can make them better for us by using coconut to replace other fats and flours. We are incredibly spoiled for choice here: tomatoes in January, strawberries all year long, inexpensive meat and vegetables galore. I would love it if you would buy the best you can afford and try to buy local produce in season. Above all, get into the kitchen and cook something!

My Pantry Staples

COCONUT (SHREDDED OR FLAKED)

Whether shredded or flaked, coconut is packed with healthy fats, fiber, and minerals. It's also low in carbohydrates and naturally low in sugar, making it a healthy addition to any dish. In the recipes in this book I've used only unsweetened coconut, even for desserts. I like to know exactly how much sugar I'm adding to my food. Also, there is a natural sweetness in coconut that goes well in sweet and savory recipes.

COCONUT OIL (REFINED OR EXPELLER-PRESSED)

Refined or expeller-pressed coconut oil is a white solid fat that generally comes in a jar. It has been chemically extracted from fresh coconut and as a result does not have a coconut flavor. It stays solid at room temperature—in fact until it reaches 77°F (25°C), when it turns into a clear liquid. Refined or expeller-pressed oil is good for deep-frying, and that's how I recommend using it, for the most part, as it's cheaper than its virgin or extra-virgin counter-part. If you can afford to, it's best to use virgin coconut oil for other cooking, or choose organic expeller-pressed oil to avoid the chemicals often used in extraction.

COCONUT OIL (EXTRA-VIRGIN OR VIRGIN)

Virgin coconut oil has a different extraction method than refined oil. Cold pressing preserves the delicate coconut flavor, and does not require any chemicals. Virgin oil is a stable fat that can be stored for a long time at room temperature. It stays solid until it reaches 77°F (25°C). I use virgin oil in almost every recipe, since most recipes don't call for much oil and the faint coconut flavor adds a nice note to most foods.

Measure the oil by scraping your measuring spoon over it until the spoon is overfull, then press down with your palm until the oil fills the spoon. The heat of your hand should soften it enough so that you get a fairly accurate measurement.

COCONUT MILK

While coconut oil is very predictable and dependable in its properties, coconut milk is the opposite. Because it is made by scraping the meat from fresh coconut, mixing it with water, and squeezing the resulting liquid through a fine strainer to remove the solids, every brand is different. They all contain different amounts of coconut fat, and many contain stabilizers.

Note that, unless otherwise specified, the recipes in this book use full-fat coconut milk.

In the can, the coconut cream (the thick white part) and the water tend to separate, so you must shake the can before opening it—unless a recipe specifies not to. This will blend the cream and the water. If the cream is too thick to be shaken, open the can and stir the cream and water until you have a homogenous mixture before adding to a recipe. I use full-fat coconut milk for pretty much every recipe, since it contains more coconut and less stabilizer.

If you don't shake or stir the can, you can spoon the coconut cream from the top and substitute it, measure for measure, for dairy cream in many recipes. It should not separate when boiled and generally has about the same fat content as whipping cream, about 35%.

COCONUT WATER

Healthier than every sports drink on the market, coconut water is nature's electrolyte drink. It has a perfect balance of potassium, sodium, and sugars and is easily absorbed by your body. It comes from the hollow center of the coconut and has a mild, sweet, and slightly nutty flavor.

COCONUT SUGAR

This sweetener is made from the sap of the coconut palm tree and has a pleasant caramel flavor. It can be substituted for brown sugar one-to-one. It contains potassium, iron, zinc, and B vitamins and has a low glycemic index rating, making it much healthier than cane sugar. Sometimes I use other sweeteners in recipes for flavor, but for the most part (with the exception of icing sugar) you should be able to successfully substitute coconut sugar in any recipe.

COCONUT FLOUR

Coconut flour is the by-product of making coconut milk; the leftover solids are defatted and ground into flour. It has no gluten and lots of fiber and is low in digestible carbohydrates. It has a mild coconut flavor and slightly grainy texture. As it's very dense, it cannot be used measure for measure to replace wheat or other flours but can be added to recipes in small amounts to increase their fiber content. It's a good flour to use for coating or dredging chicken, fish, or fritters.

BROWN RICE FLOUR

I know it's not coconut, but I find brown rice flour to be the best overall flour to use in gluten-free baking. And it's much cheaper than those gluten-free blends. Brown rice flour makes light baked goods, and is high in fiber and iron and lots of trace minerals our bodies need. It can be used to thicken sauces and is the perfect gluten-free alternative for quick breads.

ALMOND FLOUR

Finely ground almonds—also known as almond meal—are the perfect foil for the lightness of brown rice flour. In combination they produce baked goods that are moist without being heavy. Almond flour is low carb as well as a great source of protein. Because of its high fat content, it should be stored in your refrigerator or freezer if you don't think you will get through it quickly. Although the names are often used interchangeably, almond flour is often more finely ground than almond meal. As well, most products labeled almond flour are made with blanched nuts, whereas those labeled almond meal can be blanched or unblanched.

SEA SALT

In my recipes I specify using sea salt. Sea salt is made by evaporating sea water, and so it contains a ton of trace minerals. It also has a milder, almost sweeter flavor than table salt. If you do use normal table salt, use less than the amount of sea salt I call for in a recipe. Sea salt may seem expensive, but it goes a long way, and your finished dish is, as they say, only as good as your ingredients. I do suggest you try cooking with a nice fine sea salt, and which brand you buy is up to you.

AGAVE NECTAR

This sweetener is made by extracting the sap from the agave plant (the same plant that tequila is made from) and processing it until it becomes a thin syrup. It adds sweetness to recipes without adding a lot of flavor, and its runny consistency means it dissolves quickly into whatever recipe you are making. Substitute maple syrup if you don't mind the maple flavor in your recipe.

XANTHAN GUM

This is a widely used food thickener that is extracted from yeast. It is frequently used in gluten-free baking to hold tiny particles of food together much the way gluten would. I've used it only in the strawberry ice cream recipe, but because it's uncommon, I thought I should include it here. It is becoming more readily available as more people adopt gluten-free diets.

Kitchen Equipment

None of the recipes in this book require any unusual or hard-to-find equipment, but here are some tools that I've found make my own cooking easier. I've listed them in order of what I think is their importance.

KNIVES

A sharp, not too big, and comfortable knife—and the skills to use it—can be a game changer in the kitchen. Your basic arsenal should consist of three knives, and they should be the best you can afford. The first is a chef's knife, or my personal choice, a Japanese Santoku knife, with a blade about 7 or 8 inches (18 to 20 cm) long. This will be your go-to knife in the kitchen and is good for everything from chopping vegetables to carving a turkey. Get comfortable with it. Watch a video on how to use it, and practice. I think good knife skills can take cooking from a chore to a pleasure and be the difference between a half-hour prep and a full hour.

A paring knife is also very useful, but you will use it less. A 4-inch (10 cm) blade is plenty, and it can be used for finer cutting and when you might hold something in your hand to cut—the tops off beets, for example, or for getting the root bit off a garlic clove so you can peel it easily.

Both these knives require a good sharpener, and there are many on the market. Sharpening stones are for people who really know how to use them, and for the rest of us I would suggest a hand-held, ceramic-wheeled hone. Use it gently but frequently. This, plus careful storage (on a magnetic bar or in a knife block, so the sharp edges don't bang against other utensils and get blunt), should keep your knives sharp for years.

A good serrated knife is also essential for cutting baked goods without tearing or squishing them. You can't really sharpen these, but if you don't use them for anything they aren't meant for, they should last a long time.

NONSTICK PAN

Buy a good one (preferably an eco one that will not emit harmful chemicals or blister when heated over 400°F/200°C) and treat it with respect. A large and a small one would be great to have, but go big if you're getting only one. Keeping the heat around medium to medium-high and not screamingly hot should make it last a long time. That and careful washing without abrasives. I use metal utensils—carefully—in mine and it's still in good shape.

TONGS

As a professional cook, I used these so much they became an extension of my hands, and I cannot imagine cooking without them. Relatively inexpensive, the kind that have rubber non-slip handles and a latch to keep them closed in the drawer are the best. Start using them and you'll see how quick and easy it is to turn meats, roasting vegetables, and fish fingers, to move things around a hot pan, and to transfer the cooked foods to plates.

PARCHMENT PAPER

I generally don't believe in using a lot of plastic wrap or aluminum foil, and I can't stand not to reuse a perfectly good plastic bag for something. Parchment paper is something I do use, though. It replaces unhealthy cooking sprays and can make cleanup really quick. You can even use it to make muffin liners if you run out. And it can be recycled. Good stuff!

Y-PEELER

Kitchen work is all about speed and ease, and a good, sharp Y-peeler will come in handy in so many ways. Easier to hold than a straight peeler, Y-peelers can be put to use beyond peeling carrots. They go beyond the knife, making quick, consistent work of shaving hard cheese, making vegetable ribbons, zesting citrus fruits, and shaving fresh coconut. There is no real way that I know of to sharpen these, but they are cheap to replace. My best care advice is to wash and dry well immediately after use.

IMMERSION BLENDER

Indispensible in the kitchen, these can often go where blenders can't. You can (carefully) purée a soup still in its pot or make salad dressings and smoothies in an instant without having to take apart and wash up a blender. They are cheap and small, and you will use the heck out of it. I'd recommend one that comes apart into two pieces, so you can thoroughly wash the business end. *Do not* forget to unplug it first.

STAND MIXER OR HAND MIXER

If you've ever tried to whip anything to soft peaks by hand, you'll know a mixer is an important piece of equipment. Choose which-ever you have room to store. For almost every application, except heavy dough kneading, they are interchangeable.

FOOD PROCESSOR OR MINI CHOPPER

Buy whichever you have room for. These appliances mix and chop and grate in seconds, saving you hours of time in food prep. It may seem like a drag to pull one out of the cupboard, but it's indispen-sible for fine chopping, and the blade and bowl can be chucked in the dishwasher. Some things, like nut butters, really can't be made without one of these.

Breakfasts and Snacks

RECIPES

Fruit Salad with Vanilla Whipped Coconut and Coconut Chips

SERVES 4 TO 6

This is a very pretty brunch salad. The whipped coconut and the fruit salad can be made ahead and kept in the fridge overnight. The coconut chips and the whipped coconut can be used to top desserts, and the chips can be eaten by the handful as a snack. Store the chips in an airtight container.

{ DAIRY-FREE * GLUTEN-FREE * VEGAN }

1. **MAKE THE COCONUT CHIPS** Heat a small nonstick frying pan over medium-high heat. Stir in coconut and sugar; cook, stirring often, until coconut is golden brown. Sprinkle with salt and set aside to cool.

2. **MAKE THE WHIPPED COCONUT** Using an electric mixer, in a large nonplastic bowl, whip coconut cream, icing sugar, vanilla, and salt until thick and creamy (for best results, refrigerate coconut cream in the can for at least an hour). This should take about 2 minutes. Spoon into a serving bowl.

3. **ASSEMBLE THE SALAD** Peel the grapefruits and orange, removing any thick white pith, and slice them into ⅛-inch (3 mm) slices. Discard any seeds. Arrange on a platter and scatter the blackberries (if using) over top.

4. Just before serving, sprinkle the coconut chips over the salad or put them in a serving bowl to pass separately. Serve salad with the whipped coconut cream.

FOR THE COCONUT CHIPS
1 cup (250 mL) unsweetened flaked coconut
1 Tbsp (15 mL) white sugar
Pinch of salt

FOR THE WHIPPED COCONUT
½ cup (125 mL) coconut cream (scooped from the top of an unshaken chilled can of milk)
1 Tbsp (15 mL) icing sugar (gluten-free, if required)
1 tsp (5 mL) vanilla extract (or ½ vanilla bean, scraped)
⅛ tsp (0.5 mL) sea salt

FOR THE FRUIT SALAD
1 pink grapefruit
1 ruby red grapefruit
1 navel orange
½ cup (125 mL) blackberries, halved (optional)

Banana Coconut Ricotta Pancakes

MAKES 10 TO 12 SMALL PANCAKES

These pancakes are very light, though they have quite a bit of fiber per serving. I don't believe you could tell these are gluten-free unless you make them bigger than 4 or 5 inches. If they're too big, they'll break apart when you try to flip them.

························{ GLUTEN-FREE }························

3 eggs

1 tsp (5 mL) coconut sugar

½ tsp (2 mL) sea salt

1 cup (250 mL) brown rice flour

½ cup (125 mL) ricotta cheese

1 tsp (5 mL) vanilla extract

½ tsp (2 mL) baking powder

½ to ⅔ cup (125 to 150 mL) unsweetened coconut water

¼ cup (60 mL) unsweetened shredded coconut

Coconut oil, for pan

2 bananas, cut in ¼-inch (5 mm) slices (optional)

1. Preheat oven to 250°F (120°C).

2. In a large bowl, whisk eggs with sugar and salt until frothy. Stir in brown rice flour, ricotta, vanilla, and baking powder.

3. Stir in coconut water until batter is the consistency of very thick cream, then stir in shredded coconut.

4. In a large nonstick pan over medium heat, melt enough coconut oil to just coat the bottom of the pan.

5. Pour about ⅓ cup (75 mL) batter into pan for each pancake. Place 3 banana slices (if using) on top of each pancake. When edges are golden, flip pancakes. Cook until the underside is golden. Transfer to a baking sheet and keep warm in the oven. Continue with remaining batter, adding more coconut oil to the pan between batches if needed. Serve with maple syrup.

Custardy French Toast with Blueberry Maple Syrup

SERVES 4 LAVISHLY OR 6 MODESTLY

The word *custardy* perfectly describes this French toast. The coconut milk mixture soaks into the bread and gives it a light and silky texture on the inside. The inherent sweetness of the coconut milk does away with the need for additional sugar, and the blueberries cut a bit of the syrup's sweetness without obscuring its flavor. More than the sum of its not many parts. A nonstick pan is essential.

{ DAIRY-FREE }

1. Preheat oven to 200°F (100°C).

2. **MAKE THE SYRUP** Combine blueberries and maple syrup in a small pot. Heat gently over medium-low heat until berries are thawed (if frozen) and syrup is warm.

3. **MAKE THE FRENCH TOAST** In a large bowl, whisk together coconut milk, eggs, and salt until well combined. Soak each slice of bread in this mixture for at least a minute, flipping at least once.

4. In a large nonstick frying pan over medium-low heat, melt about 1 tsp (5 mL) coconut oil. When the pan is hot, fry toast in batches, flipping once, until golden brown on both sides. Remove to a baking sheet and keep warm in the oven while you make the remaining French toast. Add more coconut oil to the pan between batches if needed.

FOR THE SYRUP

1 cup (250 mL) fresh or
  frozen wild blueberries

½ cup (125 mL) maple syrup

FOR THE FRENCH TOAST

1 can (14 oz/400 mL)
  coconut milk, shaken

5 eggs

½ tsp (2 mL) sea salt

1 loaf egg bread or Italian loaf,
  sliced about ¾ inch (2 cm)
  thick

Coconut oil, for pan

Cashew Quinoa Breakfast Bars

MAKES 12 BARS OR 16 (2-INCH/5 CM) SQUARES

These bars are much less expensive and much healthier than most store-bought energy bars. You can substitute any puffed grain or seed for the puffed quinoa. You might need to wrap the bars individually to keep from eating the whole pan!

······················· { DAIRY-FREE * GLUTEN-FREE * VEGAN } ·······················

FOR THE TOPPING
1½ cups (375 mL) unsweetened shredded coconut
¼ cup (60 mL) coconut oil
1 tsp (5 mL) maple syrup

FOR THE BARS
¾ cup (175 mL) almond butter
¼ cup (60 mL) maple syrup
2 Tbsp (30 mL) coconut oil
1 cup (250 mL) puffed quinoa
¾ cup (175 mL) salted roasted cashews, coarsely chopped
½ cup (125 mL) chopped pitted dates
2 tsp (10 mL) vanilla extract
½ tsp (2 mL) sea salt

1. Line an 8-inch (2 L) square cake pan with parchment paper, leaving an inch (2.5 cm) overhang on 2 opposite sides to help lift squares out of pan.

2. **MAKE THE TOPPING** In a small frying pan over medium heat, combine coconut and coconut oil. Cook, stirring often, until coconut oil is melted and coconut is light golden brown. Remove from heat and stir in maple syrup. Set aside.

3. **MAKE THE BARS** In a medium saucepan over medium-low heat, combine almond butter, maple syrup, and coconut oil. Cook, stirring often, until almond butter and coconut oil are just melted, about 5 minutes.

4. Take pot off heat and add puffed quinoa, cashews, dates, vanilla, and salt. Stir until quinoa and cashews are evenly coated with almond butter mixture.

5. Press mixture into prepared pan. Top with coconut topping and press well with the back of a large spoon or a spatula.

6. Refrigerate until firm, at least 1 hour, then cut into squares. Store in an airtight container. These might go soft if it's really hot out, so refrigerate in summer.

Toasty Spiced Grain-Free Granola

MAKES ABOUT 3½ CUPS (875 ML)

You might not expect to find some of these spices in a granola, but they give the end result a warm and toasty flavor without being spicy. A great way to kick-start your day! Eat it by the handful, or in a bowl with your favorite milk, or sprinkled on top of your favorite hot or cold cereal. It has loads of protein and fiber. And it tastes great.

········{ DAIRY-FREE * GLUTEN-FREE * VEGAN }········

1. Preheat oven to 325°F (160°C) and generously coat a baking sheet with the coconut oil. It does not have to be an even layer.

2. In a medium bowl, combine coconut, walnuts, sunflower seeds, pumpkin seeds, sesame seeds, almonds, sugar, cinnamon, cumin, cayenne, and salt. Mix well. Spread in an even layer on oiled baking sheet.

3. Bake for 10 minutes, then stir. Bake for a further 10 minutes, stirring at least one more time. Granola is done when the coconut is lightly toasted. Let cool completely on the baking sheet. Store in an airtight container.

2 Tbsp (30 mL) coconut oil

1 cup (250 mL) unsweetened flaked or shredded coconut

1 cup (250 mL) walnut pieces or chopped walnuts

½ cup (125 mL) unsalted raw sunflower seeds

⅓ cup (75 mL) unsalted raw pumpkin seeds (pepitas)

⅓ cup (75 mL) sesame seeds

⅓ cup (75 mL) sliced almonds

2 Tbsp (30 mL) coconut sugar

1 tsp (5 mL) cinnamon

½ tsp (2 mL) ground cumin

½ tsp (2 mL) cayenne pepper

¼ tsp (1 mL) sea salt

Quinoa Porridge

SERVES 4

Porridge might be the most comforting winter breakfast there is, and quinoa makes a filling and satisfying alternative to oatmeal. Cooking the quinoa in coconut water gives it a light sweetness.

···································· { DAIRY-FREE • GLUTEN-FREE } ····································

FOR THE QUINOA

½ cup (125 mL) quinoa, rinsed and drained

1 cup (250 mL) unsweetened coconut water

2 Tbsp (30 mL) unsweetened desiccated coconut

1 Tbsp (15 mL) coconut oil

½ tsp (2 mL) sea salt

FOR THE SPICED FRUIT AND NUTS

1 Tbsp (15 mL) coconut oil

1 Tbsp (15 mL) honey

¼ tsp (1 mL) cinnamon

¼ tsp (1 mL) ground ginger

4 dried figs, quartered

A handful of dried apricots, coarsely chopped

¼ cup (60 mL) chopped walnuts

1. **MAKE THE QUINOA** In a medium saucepan, combine quinoa, coconut water, coconut, coconut oil, and salt. Bring to a boil, then reduce to a simmer and cook until quinoa is almost soft and coconut water is absorbed, about 15 minutes. Remove from heat and let rest for a few minutes.

2. **MAKE THE SPICED FRUIT AND NUTS** In a small frying pan, combine coconut oil, honey, cinnamon, and ginger. Heat over medium heat, stirring, until coconut oil is melted and mixture is combined.

3. Stir in figs, apricots, and walnuts; toss to coat.

4. Divide quinoa among bowls and top with the fruit and nuts. Serve with milk of your choice.

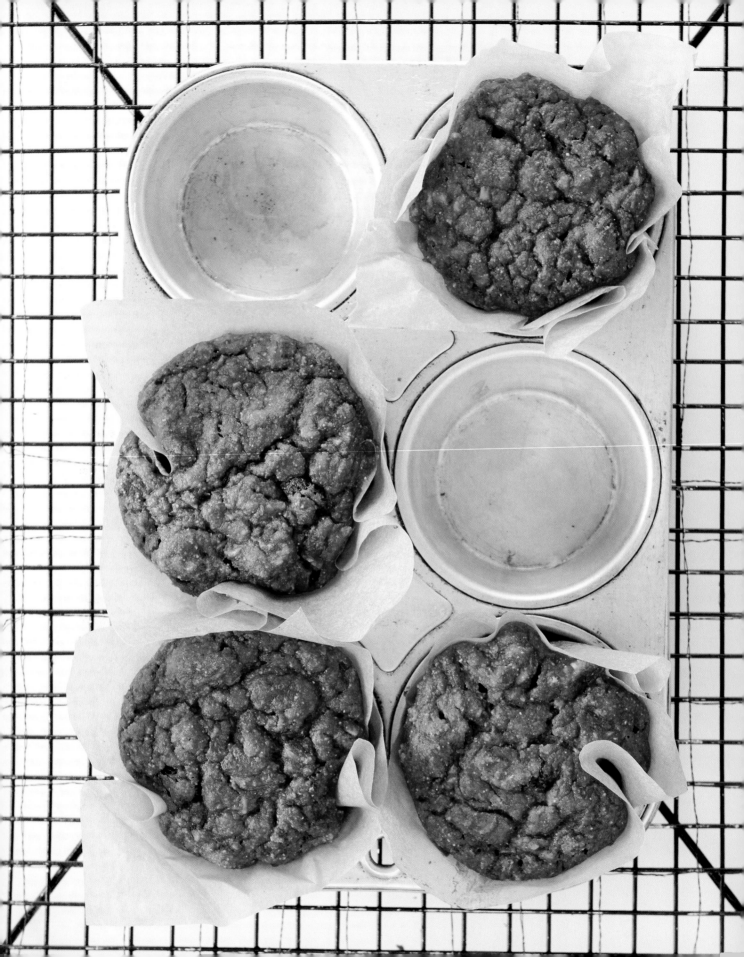

Pumpkin Spice Muffins

MAKES 12 MUFFINS

This recipe took time to perfect, but the result is, I think, worth it. These delicious muffins are healthy and gluten-free, moist and light all at the same time. My first batch stuck like crazy in the pan, so I learned that it is crucial to use paper cupcake liners or small squares of parchment to prevent sticking.

{ DAIRY-FREE • GLUTEN-FREE }

1. Preheat oven to 350°F (180°C) and line a 12-cup muffin pan with paper liners.

2. In a small saucepan over medium heat, combine coconut and coconut oil. Cook, stirring often, until coconut is golden brown. Remove from heat and set aside.

3. In a large bowl, whisk together pumpkin purée, coconut milk, eggs, coconut sugar, maple syrup, and sea salt until smooth.

4. Stir in pecan pieces, raisins, brown rice flour, toasted coconut, cornmeal, baking powder, pumpkin pie spice, and baking soda.

5. Divide batter evenly among muffin cups. Bake for 30 to 35 minutes or until a toothpick inserted in the center of a muffin comes out clean.

6. Let cool in pan for at least 15 minutes, then turn muffins out on a rack and let cool completely.

½ cup (125 mL) unsweetened shredded coconut

1 Tbsp (15 mL) coconut oil

1 can (14 oz/398 mL) pumpkin purée

½ cup (125 mL) coconut milk

3 eggs

½ cup (125 mL) coconut sugar

2 Tbsp (30 mL) maple syrup

1½ tsp (7 mL) sea salt

1 cup (250 mL) pecan pieces

½ cup (125 mL) raisins

½ cup (125 mL) brown rice flour

⅓ cup (75 mL) fine cornmeal

1½ tsp (7 mL) baking powder

1 tsp (5 mL) pumpkin pie spice

½ tsp (2 mL) baking soda

Banana Bread with Peanut Butter Swirl

MAKES 1 LOAF

Gluten-free baking is much easier than baking with wheat flour, since you don't need to worry about overmixing. (Making quick breads is one area of cooking where it helps to be lazy—you stir the ingredients just until they're combined.) This is a very good breakfast loaf, loaded with protein and fiber and not overly sweet.

·· { DAIRY-FREE ∗ GLUTEN-FREE } ··

FOR THE PEANUT BUTTER SWIRL

½ cup (125 mL) peanut butter

2 Tbsp (30 mL) honey

1 Tbsp (15 mL) coconut oil

¼ tsp (1 mL) sea salt

FOR THE BREAD

⅔ cup (150 mL) almond flour

⅔ cup (150 mL) brown rice flour

2 Tbsp (30 mL) coconut flour

4 very ripe bananas, mashed

3 eggs, lightly beaten

¼ cup (60 mL) coconut oil, melted

2 Tbsp (30 mL) honey

1½ tsp (7 mL) baking powder

½ tsp (2 mL) baking soda

½ tsp (2 mL) sea salt

1. Preheat oven to 350°F (180°C) and grease an 8- × 4-inch (1.5 L) loaf pan with coconut oil.

2. **MAKE THE PEANUT BUTTER SWIRL** In a small saucepan, combine peanut butter, honey, coconut oil, and salt. Melt over very low heat, stirring occasionally. Set aside.

3. **MAKE THE BREAD** In a large bowl, stir together almond flour, brown rice flour, coconut flour, bananas, eggs, coconut oil, honey, baking powder, baking soda, and salt until combined.

4. Fold in peanut butter mixture just enough to make a swirl throughout the batter, then pour into greased loaf pan.

5. Bake for 45 to 50 minutes or until a toothpick inserted in the bread comes out clean. Let cool in pan for about 10 minutes, then turn out on a rack and let cool completely.

Blueberry Lemon Loaf

This loaf has a light texture and bright flavor. It's not too sweet, so it's great to make for breakfasts on the go. The toasted coconut adds not only flavor but also fiber and vitamins.

························· { DAIRY-FREE * GLUTEN-FREE } ·························

1. Preheat oven to 350°F (180°C) and grease an 8- × 4-inch (1.5 L) loaf pan with coconut oil.

2. Combine coconut oil and coconut in a small frying pan. Heat over medium heat, stirring often, until coconut becomes light golden brown. Set aside to cool slightly.

3. In a large bowl, stir together brown rice flour, almond flour, baking powder, and salt. Add apple and toss until the pieces are evenly coated.

4. Stir in reserved toasted coconut, eggs, and maple syrup, then fold in blueberries and lemon zest. Pour batter into greased loaf pan.

5. Bake for 20 minutes. Reduce heat to 325°F (160°C) and bake for an additional 20 minutes or until a toothpick inserted in the center of loaf comes out clean.

6. Let cool in pan for about 10 minutes, then turn loaf out on a rack and let cool completely.

⅓ cup (75 mL) coconut oil, plus extra for pan

⅓ cup (75 mL) unsweetened desiccated coconut

⅔ cup (150 mL) brown rice flour

½ cup (125 mL) almond flour

1 tsp (5 mL) baking powder

½ tsp (2 mL) sea salt

1 medium apple, peeled and grated or finely chopped

3 eggs, lightly beaten

⅓ cup (75 mL) maple syrup

¾ cup (175 mL) fresh blueberries

1 Tbsp (15 mL) lemon zest

Fruit and Nut Butter

MAKES ABOUT 1 CUP (250 ML) SPREAD OR ABOUT 20 BALLS

Peanut butter is good, but this fruit and nut butter is far better.
It's loaded with healthy fats from the walnuts and cashews plus fiber
from the dates. Spread it on whatever you like to toast in the morning.
It's also delicious on crackers, apple slices, and celery sticks. For a
great on-the-go breakfast or snack, roll the mixture into 1-inch
(2.5 cm) balls, then roll in shredded coconut. Refrigerate until firm.

{ DAIRY-FREE • GLUTEN-FREE • VEGAN }

⅓ cup (75 mL) walnuts

⅓ cup (75 mL) raw cashews

2 Tbsp (30 mL) unsweetened shredded coconut

¼ tsp (1 mL) sea salt

4 Medjool dates, pitted

3 Tbsp (45 mL) coconut oil

½ cup (125 mL) natural peanut butter, or any nut butter of your choice

⅓ cup (75 mL) unsweetened shredded coconut, for rolling (optional)

1. In a food processor, combine walnuts, cashews, coconut, and salt. Process for about 1 minute or until very finely ground.

2. Add dates and process for another minute until they are finely chopped.

3. Scrape down sides of bowl, then add coconut oil and peanut butter. Process for another minute or so until you have a smooth paste.

4. Transfer to a jar. Or refrigerate until firm enough to handle, roll into 1-inch (2.5 cm) balls, and roll in coconut, if desired. Butter keeps, refrigerated, for 2 weeks.

Baked Eggs with Feta and Dill

SERVES 4

This pretty dish is really easy to make. If you want to serve this for brunch, you can make the feta cream in advance and bring it to room temperature before using. This also makes a quick dinner for two if you use two eggs per person and divide the ingredients between two ramekins instead of four.

················{ GLUTEN-FREE }················

FOR THE FETA CREAM
¾ cup (175 mL) coconut milk
2 oz (55 g) feta cheese, crumbled
¼ cup (60 mL) grated Parmesan cheese (optional)
½ tsp (2 mL) sea salt

FOR THE EGGS
4 eggs
1 green onion, halved lengthwise and cut in 1-inch (2.5 cm) pieces
A few sprigs fresh dill
2½ cups (625 mL) lightly packed baby spinach
Lemon wedges, for serving
Freshly ground pepper

1. Preheat oven to 300°F (150°C) and grease 4 shallow ovenproof 1-cup (250 mL) ramekins with coconut oil. Place them on a baking sheet.

2. **MAKE THE FETA CREAM** In a small bowl, combine coconut milk, feta, Parmesan (if using), and salt. Stir well.

3. **PREPARE THE EGGS** Crack 1 egg into each ramekin. Spoon one-quarter of the feta cream over each egg white. Do not cover the egg yolk. Top each ramekin with a few pieces of green onion.

4. Bake until the whites are just set and yolks are still runny, about 15 minutes.

5. Top each dish with a few sprigs of dill and a handful of spinach. Serve eggs with a wedge of lemon and lots of pepper.

Soft Scrambled Eggs with Creamed Spinach and Smoked Salmon

SERVES 4

These eggs are quick to make and have lots of flavor.
Omit the salmon for a vegetarian option.

{ DAIRY-FREE • GLUTEN-FREE }

1. **MAKE THE SPINACH** Heat olive oil in a large nonstick frying pan over medium-high heat. When oil just starts to shimmer, stir in spinach and salt; cook, stirring, until spinach is wilted and pan is dry.

2. Pour in coconut milk and lemon juice. Simmer until coconut milk thickens slightly, about 1 minute. Pour spinach into a bowl and keep warm. Wipe out pan.

3. **PREPARE THE EGGS** In a medium bowl, whisk together eggs, coconut milk, and salt until very well blended. Melt coconut oil in the frying pan over medium heat. Add egg mixture. Cook, stirring often, until eggs are just set but still creamy. Remove from pan immediately.

4. To serve, divide spinach mixture among plates and top each with a quarter of the scrambled eggs. Fold a slice of smoked salmon on top of each serving and garnish with a lemon wedge, dill, and red onion.

FOR THE SPINACH

1 tsp (5 mL) extra-virgin olive oil

6 cups (1 L) packed
baby spinach or a 5 oz
(142 g) package

¼ tsp (1 mL) sea salt

¼ cup (60 mL) coconut milk

1 tsp (5 mL) lemon juice

FOR THE EGGS

6 eggs

⅓ cup (75 mL) coconut milk

1 tsp (5 mL) sea salt

1 tsp (5 mL) coconut oil

TO SERVE

4 oz (115 g) smoked salmon

4 lemon wedges

A few sprigs fresh dill

A few thin slices red onion

Brain Power Smoothie

Blueberries and cherries are good for the brain and so are walnuts. I prefer frozen wild blueberries over fresh cultivated—the color alone tells me they are healthier.

· { DAIRY-FREE · GLUTEN-FREE · VEGAN } ·

½ cup (125 mL) coconut milk

¼ cup (60 mL) frozen blueberries

¼ cup (60 mL) frozen sweet cherries

2 Tbsp (30 mL) walnut pieces

½ tsp (2 mL) maple syrup, or more to taste

1. In a blender (or using an immersion blender), combine coconut milk, blueberries, cherries, walnuts, and maple syrup. Blend until smooth.

Coconut Date Almond Smoothie

This smoothie is *so* good for you, and so satisfying. The warming flavors make it a good winter drink. Leave out the maple syrup if you prefer a less sweet smoothie.

{ DAIRY-FREE ∘ GLUTEN-FREE ∘ VEGAN }

1. In a blender (or using an immersion blender), combine dates, banana, coconut milk, water, almond butter, maple syrup (if using), cinnamon, and ice. Blend until smooth.

2 Medjool dates, pitted

½ frozen banana

½ cup (125 mL) coconut milk

¼ cup (60 mL) water

1 Tbsp (15 mL) almond butter

1 tsp (5 mL) maple syrup (optional)

¼ tsp (1 mL) cinnamon

A handful of ice cubes

Appetizers

RECITES

Sweet-and-Spicy Popcorn

MAKES 12 TO 14 CUPS (2.8 TO 3.2 L)

Popcorn seems to be the latest thing in snack foods. There are loads of choices in the grocery store, but this recipe is healthier and quick to pull together. The secret ingredient (coconut oil) adds a subtle flavor that people can't quite put their finger on—and it makes this popcorn addictive. Dig out your popcorn poppers!

· { DAIRY-FREE ∗ GLUTEN-FREE ∗ VEGAN (OPTION) } ·

1. Place popped corn in a large bowl.

2. **MAKE THE TOPPING** In a small saucepan over low heat, combine coconut oil and butter (or additional oil). Heat, stirring occasionally, until coconut oil and butter are melted. Remove from heat and stir in sugar, cayenne pepper, and salt. Sugar will not melt.

3. Pour mixture in a thin stream over popped corn, stirring constantly until kernels are evenly coated. Store in an airtight container.

12 to 14 cups (2.8 to 3.2 L) air-popped corn (from about ⅓ cup/75 mL kernels)

FOR THE TOPPING
2 Tbsp (30 mL) coconut oil
1 Tbsp (15 mL) butter (or 1 Tbsp/15 mL coconut oil)
2 Tbsp (30 mL) coconut sugar
1½ tsp (7 mL) cayenne pepper
½ tsp (2 mL) sea salt

Sweet-and-Salty Almonds

MAKES 1½ CUPS (375 ML)

A quarter cup may seem like a lot of rosemary, a herb that is usually used sparingly. But because you add it at the beginning of this recipe, it goes crisp and a bit sweet instead of overpowering the flavor of the nuts. A revelation! If you cannot find Marcona almonds, use blanched almonds, walnuts, or a mix.

·····················{ DAIRY-FREE ∗ GLUTEN-FREE ∗ VEGAN }·····················

1½ cups (375 mL) Marcona almonds

¼ cup (60 mL) shredded unsweetened coconut

¼ cup (60 mL) fresh rosemary leaves

1 tsp (5 mL) coconut sugar

1 tsp (5 mL) coconut oil

½ tsp (2 mL) sea salt

A generous grind of pepper

1. In a small nonstick frying pan, combine almonds, coconut, rosemary, coconut sugar, coconut oil, salt, and pepper. Cook, stirring often, over medium-high heat until almonds are evenly coated and very lightly toasted, about 3 minutes.

2. Pour onto a large plate, spread in a single layer, and let cool before serving. Store in an airtight container.

Beet Hummus

MAKES 1½ TO 2 CUPS (375 TO 500 ML)

This combination of beets and tahini is great, and the addition of coconut milk lends a richness that the dip would otherwise not have. For a really wonderful appetizer, serve the hummus with sourdough bread, grilled and brushed with a little olive oil. Something magic happens between the char of the bread and the sweetness of the beets.

···{ DAIRY-FREE ∗ GLUTEN-FREE ∗ VEGAN }·····························

1. Preheat oven to 425°F (220°C).

2. **PREPARE THE BEETS** Place beets in a cast-iron frying pan or baking pan just large enough to hold them. Pour over the water. Cover the pan tightly with foil and roast beets until a sharp knife pierces them easily, 45 to 55 minutes. The water may dry up while the beets are roasting but this does not matter.

3. Uncover and let sit until cool enough to peel, about 10 minutes. Peels should push off with the sides of your fingers and thumbs, and you can use paper towel if you find the job too messy. Cut beets in half or in large chunks.

4. **MAKE THE HUMMUS** In a food processor, combine beets, garlic, coconut milk, almonds, tahini, coconut oil, lemon juice, vinegar, cumin, salt, and chili flakes. Pulse until well blended but not completely smooth.

5. Serve with toasted bread, feta cheese, and arugula, or with gluten-free crackers or toasted pitas.

FOR THE BEETS
1 lb (450 g) small to medium beets, washed and trimmed
1½ cups (375 mL) water

FOR THE HUMMUS
1 clove garlic, coarsely chopped
⅓ cup (75 mL) coconut milk
¼ cup (60 mL) blanched almonds
2 Tbsp (30 mL) tahini
1 Tbsp (15 mL) coconut oil
1 Tbsp (15 mL) lemon juice
1 tsp (5 mL) white vinegar
½ tsp (2 mL) ground cumin
½ tsp (2 mL) sea salt
¼ tsp (1 mL) chili flakes

Burnt Eggplant Dip

MAKES ABOUT 1 ½ CUPS (375 ML)

This dip has the power to convert people who think they hate eggplant.
It makes a delicious appetizer served with warm pita and is fantastic with grilled
lamb or as part of a Middle Eastern meal with falafel (page 161) and a chopped
salad. Don't be afraid to cook the eggplant for so long. It makes for better flavor.

························· { DAIRY-FREE * GLUTEN-FREE * VEGAN } ·························

FOR THE EGGPLANT

1 large or 2 medium eggplants

2 cloves garlic, quartered
   lengthwise

Sea salt and pepper

FOR THE TAHINI SAUCE

½ cup (125 mL) coconut milk

⅓ cup (75 mL) fresh
   parsley leaves

3 Tbsp (45 mL) tahini

4 tsp (20 mL) lemon juice

1 tsp (5 mL) ground cumin

1 tsp (5 mL) sea salt

TO SERVE

A drizzle of extra-virgin olive oil

¼ tsp (1 mL) za'atar or
   ground cumin

1. Preheat oven to 450°F (230°C).

2. **PREPARE THE EGGPLANT** Slice eggplant in half lengthwise.
   With the tip of a sharp knife, make ¼-inch (5 mm) deep
   cuts an inch (2.5 cm) or so apart in the flesh side. Insert
   garlic into a few of the slits, season eggplant with salt and
   pepper, and place skin side down on a baking sheet.

3. Roast eggplant until very soft and very dark brown on the
   flesh side, 20 to 30 minutes, depending on size of eggplants. Turn skin side up and let sit until cool enough to
   handle. Scrape the flesh and garlic out of the skins into a
   bowl. This does not have to be perfect—it's okay if some
   skin goes into the dip.

4. **MAKE THE TAHINI SAUCE** In a food processor, combine coconut
   milk, parsley, tahini, lemon juice, cumin, and salt. Blend
   until smooth, about 20 seconds. Set aside ¼ cup (60 mL) of
   this mixture.

5. Add eggplant and garlic to food processor and pulse until
   mixture is just blended. It should still have some texture.

6. To serve, pour eggplant dip into a shallow serving bowl
   and drizzle with olive oil and reserved tahini sauce. Sprinkle with za'atar. Serve with pita bread or crudités.

Roasted Red Pepper Dip

MAKES ABOUT 1 ½ CUPS (375 ML)

This is my favorite creamy, vegan red pepper dip. Ditch the
mayo-laden dips in favor of this interesting and very healthy version.
It's also great on burgers and as a sandwich spread.

··························{ DAIRY-FREE * GLUTEN-FREE * VEGAN }··························

1. Drain peppers well and pat dry with paper towel.

2. In a food processor, combine peppers, garlic, almonds,
   basil, parsley, coconut milk, coconut oil, vinegar, lemon
   juice, salt, and chili flakes. Process until dip is mostly
   smooth but still has some texture, about 30 seconds. Do
   not over-blend. Serve with gluten-free crackers, baguette,
   tortilla chips, or crudités.

1 jar (16 oz/500 mL)
   roasted red peppers

1 clove garlic, coarsely chopped

½ cup (125 mL) blanched
   almonds

¼ cup (60 mL) fresh basil
   leaves

¼ cup (60 mL) fresh
   parsley leaves

¼ cup (60 mL) coconut milk

1 Tbsp (15 mL) coconut oil

2 tsp (10 mL) balsamic vinegar

1 tsp (5 mL) lemon juice

1 tsp (5 mL) sea salt

¼ tsp (1 mL) chili flakes,
   or to taste

Coconut Shrimp

This is likely the first thing that comes to mind when you think of a savory coconut recipe. No wonder—tender shrimp with a crispy, slightly sweet and spicy coating are delicious. The small amount of cayenne delivers just a little hit of heat, so feel free to increase the amount as your taste dictates. The size of the shrimp is up to you.

······················{ DAIRY-FREE ∗ GLUTEN-FREE }·····················

1 lb (450 g) medium-large raw shrimp (26/30 or 31/35), peeled and deveined, tails left on

Coconut oil, for frying

FOR THE COATING

⅓ cup (75 mL) cornstarch

2 egg whites

Juice of 1 lime

½ tsp (2 mL) cayenne pepper, or more to taste

½ tsp (2 mL) sea salt

¾ cup (175 mL) unsweetened shredded coconut

1. **MAKE THE COATING** In a large shallow bowl, combine cornstarch, egg whites, lime juice, cayenne, and salt. Whisk with a fork until well mixed.

2. Place coconut in a second shallow bowl.

3. Dip each shrimp into egg white mixture, then press into coconut, turning, until well coated.

4. Heat ¼ inch (5 mm) coconut oil in a large nonstick frying pan over medium-high heat. When oil is shimmering, add shrimp in batches. Do not overcrowd pan.

5. Fry until coconut is golden brown and shrimp is pink, about 2 minutes per side. Drain on paper towels. Serve with mango chutney or chili sauce.

Sesame Shrimp Toasts

SERVES 6 TO 8

These light but flavor-packed appetizers get a really good crunch from the water chestnuts. You can bypass the bread and turn these into a main course by dropping the shrimp mixture by the spoonful into the sesame seeds, tossing to coat, and baking according to the directions below.

················{ DAIRY-FREE * GLUTEN-FREE (OPTION) }·····················

1. **MAKE THE SHRIMP MIXTURE** In a food processor, combine shrimp, water chestnuts, cilantro, coconut, garlic, egg, and tamari sauce. Pulse until mixture is well blended but not completely smooth. Refrigerate for at least half an hour.

2. **MEANWHILE, MAKE THE SAUCE** In a small serving bowl, combine coconut water, lime juice, fish sauce, coconut sugar, chili, cilantro, and green onion. Stir until sugar is dissolved.

3. **PREPARE THE TOASTS** Preheat oven to 400°F (200°C) and rub a baking sheet with 2 Tbsp (30 mL) coconut oil.

4. In a small saucepan over medium heat, toast sesame seeds, stirring, until golden, about 2 minutes. Transfer to a shallow bowl and set aside to cool.

5. Spread about a tablespoon (15 mL) of shrimp mixture onto each slice of bread. Dip shrimp side of bread into sesame seeds. Seeds will stick to the shrimp mixture.

6. Place toasts on prepared baking sheet and bake until shrimp mixture is firm to the touch and slightly pink, about 12 minutes. Serve hot or at room temperature, with the sauce for dipping.

FOR THE SHRIMP MIXTURE
½ lb (225 g) raw shrimp, peeled and deveined
½ cup (125 mL) drained canned sliced water chestnuts
½ cup (125 mL) coarsely chopped fresh cilantro leaves and stems
¼ cup (60 mL) unsweetened shredded coconut
4 cloves garlic, coarsely chopped
1 egg
4 tsp (20 mL) tamari soy sauce (gluten-free, if required)

FOR THE SAUCE
¼ cup (60 mL) unsweetened coconut water
2 Tbsp (30 mL) lime juice
1 Tbsp (15 mL) fish sauce (gluten-free, if required)
1 tsp (5 mL) coconut sugar
½ red chili, thinly sliced
A handful of fresh cilantro leaves
1 green onion, thinly sliced

FOR THE TOASTS
2 Tbsp (30 mL) coconut oil
¼ cup (60 mL) sesame seeds
20 slices baguette

Chicken Satays

SERVES 6 TO 8

Alchemy happens when you marinate chicken in coconut milk: the chicken becomes incredibly tender. But marinate only for the specified time, otherwise the chicken will become almost too soft. Grilling adds a lovely dimension to these appetizers, but they can also be broiled for about three minutes per side.

·······················{ DAIRY-FREE * GLUTEN-FREE }·······················

1 lb (450 g) boneless, skinless chicken breast

FOR THE MARINADE
½ cup (125 mL) peanut butter
⅓ cup (75 mL) coconut milk
2 Tbsp (30 mL) soy sauce (gluten-free, if required)
1 Tbsp (15 mL) coconut sugar
1 Tbsp (15 mL) Sriracha sauce
1 Tbsp (15 mL) fish sauce (gluten-free, if required)
1 clove garlic, coarsely chopped
Juice of 1 lime

TO SERVE
1 lime, cut in wedges
A handful of fresh cilantro leaves
1 red chili, thinly sliced

1. Soak about 20 (6-inch/15 cm) wooden skewers in cold water for at least half an hour (or use metal skewers).

2. **MAKE THE MARINADE** In a tall container, combine peanut butter, coconut milk, soy sauce, coconut sugar, Sriracha, fish sauce, garlic, and lime juice. Blend with an immersion blender. Set aside half the mixture to use as a dip. Pour remaining marinade into a medium bowl.

3. Cut chicken crosswise into ½-inch (1 cm) strips. Add chicken to marinade in bowl, turning to coat well. Let marinate, covered and refrigerated, for half an hour.

4. Preheat grill to medium-high. Oil grill.

5. Thread each piece of chicken onto a skewer. Grill satays for about 4 minutes per side or until firm and marked with grill marks. Serve with lime wedges, cilantro, chili slices, and reserved dip.

Indian-Spiced Onion Fritters with Coconut Chutney

SERVES 8 TO 10

Onions are one of the world's most versatile vegetables, and these appetizers really glorify them. South Indian spicing is quite different from North Indian—fresh and light with a good spice level that balances out the sting from the onions, and the chutney is a cooling (and addictive!) accompaniment. It's good served with almost anything spicy. Try it with the curried carrots on page 146 as part of an Indian feast.

·······················{ DAIRY-FREE ∗ GLUTEN-FREE ∗ VEGAN }·····················

1. Preheat oven to 250°F (120°C).

2. **MAKE THE CHUTNEY** In a tall container, combine coconut, coconut water, cilantro, ginger, lime juice, and salt. Blitz with an immersion blender until well combined. Mixture will not be perfectly smooth. Let sit for at least 10 minutes before serving so the coconut can absorb some of the liquid.

3. **MAKE THE FRITTERS** In a large bowl, stir together water, chickpea flour, brown rice flour, coconut, mustard seeds, fennel seeds, chili flakes, coriander, salt, and baking soda until well mixed. Let batter sit for about 15 minutes.

4. Stir in onions and cilantro until onions are well coated.

5. Heat about ¼ inch (5 mm) coconut oil in a large frying pan over medium-high heat. When oil is shimmering, working in batches, drop batter by the heaping tablespoon (to make a 2-inch/5 cm fritter) into oil. Fry gently until golden brown on both sides, 2 to 3 minutes per side.

6. Drain on paper towels and keep warm in the oven while you repeat with the rest of the batter. Add more coconut oil to the pan if it is becoming dry.

7. Fritters can be reheated in a 350°F (180°C) oven for about 10 minutes before serving with chutney.

FOR THE CHUTNEY
½ cup (125 mL) unsweetened shredded coconut
½ cup (125 mL) unsweetened coconut water
⅓ cup (75 mL) fresh cilantro leaves
1 tsp (5 mL) grated fresh ginger
1 tsp (5 mL) lime juice
¼ tsp (1 mL) sea salt

FOR THE FRITTERS
1 cup (250 mL) cold water
½ cup (125 mL) chickpea flour
¼ cup (60 mL) brown rice flour
¼ cup (60 mL) unsweetened shredded coconut
2 Tbsp (30 mL) black mustard seeds
2 tsp (10 mL) fennel seeds
1 tsp (5 mL) chili flakes
1 tsp (5 mL) ground coriander
1 tsp (5 mL) sea salt
½ tsp (2 mL) baking soda
1 very large or 2 small white or sweet onions, quartered and sliced ⅛ inch (3 mm) thick
½ cup (125 mL) fresh cilantro leaves, chopped
Coconut oil, for frying

Garlic Bread

SERVES 4 TO 6

Coconut vinegar takes this garlic bread to a whole new dimension.
If you don't have coconut vinegar, use white wine or red wine vinegar.

···{ DAIRY-FREE * VEGAN }···

1 baguette

FOR THE SPREAD
¼ cup (60 mL) fresh
    parsley leaves
1 large clove garlic, coarsely
    chopped
3 Tbsp (45 mL) coconut oil
1 Tbsp (15 mL) extra-virgin
    olive oil
½ tsp (2 mL) coconut vinegar
¼ tsp (1 mL) chili flakes
¼ tsp (1 mL) sea salt

1. Preheat oven to 350°F (180°C).

2. Cut baguette in half horizontally, without cutting all the way through.

3. **MAKE THE SPREAD** In a tall container, combine parsley, garlic, coconut oil, olive oil, coconut vinegar, chili flakes, and salt. Blend with an immersion blender until well mixed but not completely smooth.

4. Place bread on baking sheet and spread mixture evenly on cut sides. Close bread and bake for 10 minutes. Open bread and bake until toasted, about 5 minutes.

5. Cut into 2-inch (5 cm) pieces and serve warm.

Salads and Soups

RECIPES

Vietnamese Beef Salad with Cucumber and Herbs

SERVES 4

Vietnamese food hits all the flavor notes. *Fresh* is the best word to describe this main-course salad—and *bright*, and *quite spicy*. This is the perfect dinner for a hot summer evening, as the herbs and cucumber and even the chili are incredibly cooling. If you'd prefer to keep the heat outdoors, grill the steak on a hot grill for the time specified.

· { DAIRY-FREE · GLUTEN-FREE } ·

½ lb (225 g) strip loin steak, 1 inch (2.5 cm) thick

FOR THE DRESSING
¼ cup (60 mL) unsweetened coconut water

¼ cup (60 mL) lime juice

3 Tbsp (45 mL) fish sauce (gluten-free, if required)

2 Tbsp (30 mL) finely chopped fresh cilantro stems

1 tsp (5 mL) coconut sugar

FOR THE TOPPING
3 Tbsp (45 mL) unsweetened desiccated coconut

2 Tbsp (30 mL) sesame seeds

FOR THE SALAD
½ head iceberg lettuce, chopped

2 to 3 baby cucumbers, thinly sliced

1 cup (250 mL) coarsely chopped fresh cilantro leaves

1 cup (250 mL) fresh basil leaves, coarsely chopped

½ cup (125 mL) fresh mint leaves, coarsely chopped

1 red chili, thinly sliced (this will make it HOT)

1. Place steak in a large resealable plastic bag or a shallow dish just large enough to hold it.

2. **MAKE THE DRESSING** Combine coconut water, lime juice, fish sauce, cilantro, and coconut sugar; stir until sugar is dissolved.

3. Pour ¼ cup (60 mL) dressing over steak and marinate for at least an hour or up to 2 hours. Reserve remaining dressing to dress the salad.

4. **MAKE THE TOPPING** Heat a medium frying pan over medium-high heat. Add coconut and sesame seeds; cook, stirring often, until coconut and sesame seeds are golden brown. Scrape into a small bowl and return pan to heat.

5. Drain steak, discarding marinade. When pan is hot, add steak (you should not need oil). Cook for 3 to 4 minutes on each side for medium-rare. Remove to a cutting board and let rest for about 10 minutes.

6. **JUST BEFORE SERVING, ASSEMBLE THE SALAD** On a large serving plate, toss together lettuce, cucumbers, cilantro, basil, mint, and chili slices.

7. Slice steak and arrange over the salad. Spoon reserved dressing over salad and sprinkle with toasted coconut and sesame seeds.

Caesar Salad

SERVES 4 TO 6

Crunchy leaves tossed with a tangy, creamy dressing—what's not to love?
The perfect summer salad . . . or winter, for that matter. The traditional yolk-based
dressing is considerably lightened up in this version made with coconut milk.
This salad can take lots of other additions: steamed green beans or asparagus,
marinated artichoke hearts, Belgian endive, a good grating of fresh horseradish.
I like to kick it up a notch with a few extra dashes of hot sauce.

· { DAIRY-FREE * GLUTEN-FREE * VEGAN } ·

1. **MAKE THE DRESSING** In a blender, combine garlic, coconut milk, lemon juice, Parmesan (if using), capers, olive oil, mustard, Worcestershire sauce, hot sauce, and salt. Blend until thick and creamy.

2. **ASSEMBLE THE SALAD** In a large bowl, toss dressing with romaine leaves. Arrange on a platter and top with eggs (if using) and chives. Season with pepper.

FOR THE DRESSING

1 small clove garlic

⅓ cup (75 mL) coconut milk

¼ cup (60 mL) lemon juice

⅓ cup (75 mL) grated Parmesan cheese (optional)

2 Tbsp (30 mL) capers

2 Tbsp (30 mL) extra-virgin olive oil

1 Tbsp (15 mL) Dijon mustard (gluten-free, if required)

1 Tbsp (15 mL) Worcestershire sauce or tamari soy sauce (gluten-free, if required)

¼ tsp (1 mL) hot sauce

¼ tsp (1 mL) sea salt

FOR THE SALAD

2 small heads romaine lettuce, cut in bite-sized pieces

4 hard-cooked eggs (optional)

Large handful of sliced chives

Freshly ground pepper

Tomatoes with Salad Cream

MAKES ¾ CUP (175 ML)

I once made a version of this salad dressing by mistake when I worked as a cook in a restaurant. The flavor took me instantly back to my childhood, when my mother would dress salads with the very British salad cream. Coconut milk works perfectly here, as it has just the right amount of sweetness.

···························· { DAIRY-FREE * GLUTEN-FREE * VEGAN } ····························

FOR THE DRESSING
½ cup (125 mL) coconut milk
2 Tbsp (30 mL) finely
  chopped shallot
2 Tbsp (30 mL) olive oil
2 Tbsp (30 mL) red wine vinegar
2 tsp (10 mL) Dijon mustard
  (gluten-free, if required)
¼ tsp (1 mL) sea salt
Freshly ground pepper

FOR THE SALAD
1 lb (450 g) tomatoes (any
  kind), sliced or halved
1 bunch fresh chives, snipped

1. **MAKE THE DRESSING** In a medium jar, combine coconut milk, shallot, olive oil, vinegar, mustard, salt, and pepper to taste. Shake until well mixed.

2. **ASSEMBLE THE SALAD** Arrange tomato slices or halves on a platter and sprinkle with chives. Drizzle with dressing and top with lots of freshly ground pepper.

Middle Eastern Chopped Salad with Tahini

SERVES 4

At the Middle Eastern table this salad would be many things: condiment, sandwich filler, and side. It is fresh and crunchy and has a tangy depth. The dressing can be made ahead—it improves with some time in the fridge. This salad makes a perfect vegetarian dinner served with falafel (page 161) and pickles.

{ DAIRY-FREE ◦ GLUTEN-FREE ◦ VEGAN }

1. **MAKE THE DRESSING** In a tall container, combine coconut milk, tahini, vinegar, lemon juice, parsley, garlic, salt, cumin, and pepper to taste. Blend with an immersion blender until smooth.

2. **ASSEMBLE THE SALAD** In a large bowl, combine red pepper, cucumber, shallot, and cherry tomatoes. Toss with dressing. Top with parsley leaves and za'atar.

FOR THE DRESSING

¼ cup (60 mL) coconut milk

¼ cup (60 mL) tahini

1 Tbsp (15 mL) white vinegar

Juice of ½ lemon

A handful of fresh
    parsley leaves

1 small clove garlic,
    coarsely chopped

½ tsp (2 mL) sea salt

¼ tsp (1 mL) ground cumin

Freshly ground pepper

FOR THE SALAD

1 sweet red pepper,
    coarsely chopped

½ English cucumber,
    coarsely chopped

1 large shallot, finely chopped

1 cup (250 mL) cherry
    tomatoes, halved or
    quartered

Fresh parsley leaves,
    for garnish

A few pinches of za'atar,
    for garnish

Arugula Salad with Candied Bacon, Pear, and Creamy Parmesan Dressing

SERVES 4

This is the opposite of a boring salad! It's a much lighter variation on the kind of salad that uses the bacon fat in the dressing. Here the bacon adds crunch, sweetness, and heat to a fresh combination of peppery and bitter greens and fresh, crisp pear. The dressing is creamy and flavorful. Need I say more?

· { GLUTEN-FREE } ·

FOR THE BACON

5 slices bacon, cut in ½-inch (1 cm) strips

½ tsp (2 mL) coconut sugar

⅛ tsp (0.5 mL) cayenne pepper

FOR THE DRESSING

¼ cup (60 mL) lightly packed finely grated Parmesan cheese

¼ cup (60 mL) coconut cream (scooped from the top of an unshaken chilled can of coconut milk)

4 tsp (20 mL) lemon juice

1 Tbsp (15 mL) extra-virgin olive oil

1½ tsp (7 mL) Dijon mustard (gluten-free, if required)

¼ tsp (1 mL) sea salt

FOR THE SALAD

4 big handfuls of baby arugula

1 big handful of frisée (optional)

1 Bosc pear, thinly sliced

1 shallot, thinly sliced

Fresh basil leaves (optional)

Freshly ground pepper

1. **PREPARE THE BACON** In a small nonstick frying pan over medium heat, cook bacon until almost crisp. Remove from heat and stir in coconut sugar and cayenne.

2. Using a slotted spoon, lift bacon out of pan. Drain on paper towels.

3. **MAKE THE DRESSING** In a medium jar, combine Parmesan, coconut cream, lemon juice, olive oil, mustard, and salt. Shake until combined.

4. **JUST BEFORE SERVING, ASSEMBLE THE SALAD** On a platter, toss together arugula, frisée (if using), pear, shallot, and basil (if using). Season with pepper. Drizzle with dressing and top with bacon.

Curried Chicken Salad

This quick and easy salad makes a great main course for a summer lunch or dinner. The coconut milk is a much healthier substitute for mayonnaise and adds a bit of sweetness that nicely complements the curry and fruit. The whole salad, greens included, can be piled into a pita or made into a sandwich with great success.

························{ DAIRY-FREE * GLUTEN-FREE }························

1. **MAKE THE DRESSING** In a large bowl, combine coconut milk, lemon juice, mango chutney, olive oil, curry powder, cayenne, and salt. Stir well.

2. **ASSEMBLE THE SALAD** To the dressing, add apple, celery, spinach, chicken, raisins, cilantro, cashews, and green onions. Gently stir until coated with dressing. Garnish with reserved celery leaves.

FOR THE DRESSING

½ cup (125 mL) coconut milk

Juice of ½ lemon

1 Tbsp (15 mL) mango chutney (gluten-free, if required)

1 Tbsp (15 mL) extra-virgin olive oil

2 tsp (10 mL) curry powder

½ tsp (2 mL) cayenne pepper

½ tsp (2 mL) sea salt

FOR THE SALAD

1 Granny Smith apple, cut in large dice

2 ribs celery, sliced, leaves reserved for garnish

4 cups (1 L) baby spinach

2 to 3 cups (500 to 750 mL) leftover rotisserie or roasted chicken, skin removed, cut in bite-sized pieces

⅓ cup (75 mL) raisins

⅓ cup (75 mL) chopped fresh cilantro

⅓ cup (75 mL) salted roasted cashews

2 green onions (white and green parts), thinly sliced

Quinoa Salad with Roasted Pumpkin and Feta

SERVES 4 TO 6

The sweet and spicy pumpkin and crispy coconut really liven up this hearty vegetarian salad. It makes a very satisfying lunch. The salad can be made (without the arugula) a day or two ahead and refrigerated; toss with the arugula just before serving. I love the flavor of goat's milk feta, but you can use your favorite feta, or leave it out altogether for a vegan version.

·······················{ GLUTEN-FREE * VEGAN (OPTION) }·······················

FOR THE ROASTED PUMPKIN

1 Tbsp (15 mL) coconut oil

1 small pumpkin or butternut squash (2 lb/900 g), peeled and cut in ½-inch (1 cm) pieces (about 3 cups/ 750 mL)

¾ cup (175 mL) unsweetened flaked coconut

¼ cup (60 mL) pumpkin seeds (pepitas)

½ tsp (2 mL) sweet smoked paprika

½ tsp (2 mL) ground cumin

½ tsp (2 mL) sea salt

¼ tsp (1 mL) chili flakes

FOR THE QUINOA

½ cup (125 mL) quinoa, rinsed well

1¼ cups (300 mL) chicken stock (gluten-free, if required) or water

¼ tsp (1 mL) sea salt (if using water)

FOR THE SALAD

4 cups (1 L) lightly packed baby arugula

2 to 3 oz (55 to 85 g) feta cheese, crumbled (optional)

3 green onions (white and green parts), sliced

3 Tbsp (45 mL) lemon juice

1 Tbsp (15 mL) olive oil

½ tsp (2 mL) sea salt

Freshly ground pepper

1. Preheat oven to 400°F (200°C). Line a baking sheet with parchment paper and grease parchment with the coconut oil.

2. **MAKE THE ROASTED PUMPKIN** In a large bowl or on the baking sheet, toss together pumpkin, coconut, pumpkin seeds, paprika, cumin, salt, and chili flakes. Spread in a single layer on the baking sheet and roast, stirring a couple of times, until pumpkin is tender and coconut is deep golden brown, about 15 minutes. Set aside to cool.

3. **MEANWHILE, MAKE THE QUINOA** Combine quinoa, chicken stock, and salt in a medium saucepan. Bring to a boil, then reduce heat and cover. Simmer, stirring occasionally, until quinoa is tender and water is absorbed, 17 to 20 minutes. Uncover and set aside to cool.

4. **JUST BEFORE SERVING, ASSEMBLE THE SALAD** In a large bowl, toss together arugula, feta, green onions, lemon juice, olive oil, salt, and pepper to taste. Gently stir in pumpkin mixture and

Cauliflower Soup

Simple and satisfying. There are not a lot of ingredients in this soup, but at the same time, nothing is missing. Quintessential cauliflower, earthy and creamy and with a lovely subtle sweetness.

· { DAIRY-FREE * GLUTEN-FREE * VEGAN } ·

1. In a large pot, combine leek, onion, garlic, salt, and coconut oil. Cook over medium heat, stirring often, until leeks and onions are soft and translucent but not browned.

2. Stir in cauliflower and potato, then stir in water. Bring to a boil, reduce heat, and simmer until cauliflower and potatoes are fork-tender, about 15 minutes.

3. Remove from heat and blend with an immersion blender until very smooth. Stir in lemon juice and coconut milk.

4. Just before serving, reheat gently. Do not allow to boil. Serve garnished with parsley leaves and pepper.

1 leek (white and light green part only), halved lengthwise and sliced ½ inch (1 cm) thick

1 small onion, chopped

1 clove garlic, smashed

1 Tbsp (15 mL) sea salt

1 Tbsp (15 mL) coconut oil or butter

1 head cauliflower, cut in large pieces

1 small Yukon Gold potato, peeled and diced (about ½ cup/125 mL)

4 cups (1 L) hot water

Juice of ½ lemon

½ cup (125 mL) coconut milk

Fresh parsley leaves, for garnish

Freshly ground pepper

Creamy Tomato Soup

SERVES 4

This soup can be a satisfying lunch, a simple dinner, or a fancy starter, depending on how you garnish it. Canned tomatoes are always more flavorful than pale, out-of-season fresh ones. I've specified whole tomatoes, squeezed by hand, because I think this results in better flavor and texture than canned crushed tomatoes. Kids are very good at this job, though there will be some wiping up afterwards.

···································· { DAIRY-FREE ∗ GLUTEN-FREE ∗ VEGAN } ····································

1 Tbsp (15 mL) coconut oil

1 large sprig fresh basil, leaves and stem reserved separately

2 cloves garlic, coarsely chopped

1 tsp (5 mL) salt

¼ tsp (1 mL) chili flakes

1 can (28 oz/796 mL) whole tomatoes

1 cup (250 mL) water

⅓ cup (75 mL) coconut milk

Extra-virgin olive oil, for garnish

Freshly cracked pepper

1. In a large pot over medium-low heat, melt coconut oil. Add basil stem, garlic, salt, and chili flakes. Cook, stirring often, until garlic just begins to turn golden.

2. Add tomatoes, squeezing each one as you add it to break them up (or use a fork or potato masher), then add water. Raise heat and bring to a boil, then reduce heat and simmer for about 5 minutes. Remove basil stem.

3. Reduce heat to low and stir in coconut milk; simmer just to heat through. Serve garnished with a few reserved basil leaves, a drizzle of olive oil, and pepper.

Cold Potato and Leek Soup

SERVES 4 TO 6

Here's a healthier version of the (deceivingly light-tasting) classic French vichyssoise. The fennel makes this a very refreshing and light soup for a summer dinner. It tastes better if made a day or two or in advance. It's delicious served with tomatoes with salad cream (page 76) and a fresh fruit dessert.

·······················{ DAIRY-FREE · GLUTEN-FREE }·······························

1. In a large pot, combine leeks, fennel, olive oil, and salt; stir to combine. Cook gently over medium-high heat, stirring occasionally, until leeks and fennel are soft but not browned, 8 to 10 minutes.

2. Raise heat to high. Pour in chicken stock and stir in grated potato. Bring to a boil, then reduce heat and simmer until potatoes are fork-tender, 10 to 15 minutes.

3. Purée in a blender in batches until very smooth. Transfer to a bowl and stir in coconut milk, lemon juice, and cayenne. Let cool to room temperature.

4. Refrigerate until ready to serve. Serve garnished with chives and black pepper.

4 leeks (white and light green parts), halved lengthwise and thickly sliced

1 fennel bulb, coarsely chopped (about 2 cups/500 mL)

1 Tbsp (15 mL) extra-virgin olive oil

1½ tsp (7 mL) sea salt

4 cups (1 L) chicken stock (gluten-free, if required)

1 medium Yukon Gold potato, peeled and grated

½ cup (125 mL) coconut milk

Juice of ½ lemon

¼ tsp (1 mL) cayenne pepper

¼ cup (60 mL) chopped fresh chives

Freshly cracked black pepper

Cream of Wild Mushroom Soup

SERVES 6 TO 8

Is there any food more comforting than a creamy mushroom soup?
I used to eat a canned version as a child—and loved it. This is the grown-up
version, though it is simple enough to appeal to kids. Good for winter
and satisfying as a meal with a little something else. In this recipe, coconut is
not the star. Its flavor is lost in the earthy depth of mushrooms, but its creaminess
makes for an earthy, rich, and filling—but still healthy—soup.

·················· { DAIRY-FREE ∗ GLUTEN-FREE ∗ VEGAN } ··················

2 leeks (white part only), halved
    lengthwise and sliced ¼ inch
    (5 mm) thick

2 cloves garlic, coarsely
    chopped

1 large sprig fresh thyme

1 Tbsp (15 mL) coconut oil

2 tsp (10 mL) sea salt

1 lb (450 g) assorted wild
    mushrooms, coarsely
    chopped

¼ cup (60 mL) dry white wine

4 cups (1 L) chicken stock
    (gluten-free, if required)
    or water

2 cups (500 mL) water

Juice of ½ lemon

1 cup (250 mL) coconut milk

2 tsp (10 mL) tamari soy sauce
    (gluten-free, if required)

Freshly cracked pepper

TO SERVE

Extra-virgin olive oil

Fresh thyme leaves

1. In a large pot, combine leeks, garlic, thyme sprig, coconut oil, and salt. Cook over medium heat, stirring occasionally, until leeks are soft.

2. Stir in mushrooms. Cook, stirring occasionally, until they are soft, about 5 minutes.

3. Raise heat to high and pour in wine, chicken stock, and water. Bring to a boil, reduce heat, and simmer, stirring occasionally, for about half an hour.

4. Remove from heat and stir in lemon juice, coconut milk, and tamari sauce.

5. Transfer half of soup (about 3 cups/750 mL) to a blender and blend until very smooth.

6. Return puréed soup to the pot and stir until combined. Reheat gently—do not allow to boil. Season with salt and lots of freshly cracked pepper. Serve garnished with a drizzle of olive oil and a sprinkle of thyme leaves.

Thai Coconut Chicken Soup

SERVES 4

A Thai classic, this is a quick and easy soup-as-a-meal. You do have to remove the herb stems before eating, but the aromatic ginger slices, lemongrass, and lime leaves can be picked out as you eat—that's part of the fun of eating this soup.

·······················{ DAIRY-FREE • GLUTEN-FREE }·······················

1. In a large pot, stir together chicken thighs, chicken stock, ginger, coconut sugar, basil and cilantro stems, chili, and lemongrass. Bring to a boil, then reduce heat and simmer for about 5 minutes.

2. Remove basil and cilantro stems. Stir in mushrooms, lime leaves, coconut milk, fish sauce, and lime juice. Continue to simmer gently for about 2 minutes.

3. Serve soup with bowls of cilantro leaves, basil leaves, and lime wedges on the side.

4 boneless, skinless chicken thighs (1 lb/450 g), cut in bite-sized chunks

4 cups (1 L) chicken stock (gluten-free, if required)

2-inch (5 cm) piece fresh ginger, peeled and cut in matchsticks

2 tsp (10 mL) coconut sugar

3 fresh basil stems (without leaves)

3 fresh cilantro stems (without leaves)

1 red chili, halved lengthwise

1 stalk lemongrass, halved lengthwise and cut in 2-inch (5 cm) pieces

7 oz (200 g) cremini mushrooms, halved or quartered

8 kaffir lime leaves

1 cup (250 mL) coconut milk

¼ cup (60 mL) fish sauce (gluten-free, if required)

Juice of 1 lime

TO SERVE

1 cup (250 mL) fresh cilantro leaves

1 cup (250 mL) fresh basil leaves (preferably Thai)

1 lime, cut in quarters

Red Lentil Soup with Coconut Milk

SERVES 4

I make this soup when I'm on my own for dinner, with little in the way of groceries and not much time or inclination to cook. And I always end up going back to the pot for more. This short list of ingredients turns out a very complex and delicious soup. The coconut milk adds a satisfying richness to this Middle Eastern classic. If you can't find za'atar, you can use ground cumin.

{ DAIRY-FREE • GLUTEN-FREE • VEGAN }

½ white onion, finely chopped

1½ cups (375 mL) red lentils, rinsed

½ cup (125 mL) long-grain white rice

2½ tsp (12 mL) sea salt

6 cups (1.5 L) water

¼ cup (60 mL) chopped fresh cilantro leaves

1 tsp (5 mL) ground cumin

TO SERVE

⅓ cup (75 mL) coconut milk

1 tsp (5 mL) za'atar

1 lemon, cut in wedges

1. In a large pot, combine onion, lentils, rice, salt, and water. Bring to a boil over high heat. Reduce heat to a simmer, skim off foam, and partially cover. Simmer, stirring occasionally, until lentils and rice are very tender, about 25 minutes.

2. Stir in cilantro and cumin. Taste and adjust seasoning.

3. Ladle soup into bowls and top each serving with a tablespoon or so of coconut milk and a pinch of za'atar. Serve with a wedge of lemon on the side.

Fish and Meat Mains

RECIPES

Mussels with Leeks, White Wine, and Herbs

SERVES 2 AS A MAIN COURSE OR 4 AS A STARTER

In this new take on a French classic, coconut milk replaces the less healthy cream in the flavorful winey, briny broth. Mussels are so good for you and so quick and easy to prepare. What could be better?

...........................{ DAIRY-FREE • GLUTEN-FREE }...........................

2 leeks (white and light green parts), halved lengthwise and sliced ¼ inch (5 mm) thick

½ white onion, sliced ¼ inch (5 mm) thick

3 or 4 sprigs fresh thyme

2 cloves garlic, thinly sliced

1 Tbsp (15 mL) coconut oil

1 Tbsp (15 mL) extra-virgin olive oil

1 tsp (5 mL) sea salt

½ cup (125 mL) dry white wine

½ cup (125 mL) coconut milk

2 lb (900 g) mussels, scrubbed and debearded

1. In a large pot over medium-high heat, combine leeks, onion, thyme, garlic, coconut oil, olive oil, and salt. Cook, stirring often, until leeks and onions are soft but not browned.

2. Stir in white wine and coconut milk. Bring to a boil.

3. Pour in mussels and stir. Cover and boil, stirring a couple of times, until mussels have just opened, 3 to 5 minutes. Discard any that do not open.

4. Using a slotted spoon, divide mussels among bowls, then ladle some broth over each bowl. Serve immediately.

Shrimp Tacos

MAKES ABOUT 12 TACOS

Is there anything hotter than tacos right now? This piquant shrimp version tastes fresh and light. The marinade and the sauce are one and the same, making these tacos quick to pull together. If you are feeling in an austere mood, dispense with the corn tortillas and serve the shrimp and toppings in an iceberg lettuce leaf.

···{ DAIRY-FREE ∗ GLUTEN-FREE }···

1. **MAKE THE MARINADE** In a tall container, combine coconut milk, cilantro, chipotle in adobo, olive oil, garlic, salt, and lime juice. Blend with an immersion blender until smooth.

2. Pour about ¼ cup (60 mL) marinade over shrimp in a bowl; stir until well coated. Cover and refrigerate for about 20 minutes. Set aside remaining marinade in a serving bowl.

3. **PREPARE THE TACOS** In a large nonstick frying pan over medium-high heat, warm tortillas 1 at a time. Remove to a plate as they're done and cover with a damp kitchen towel.

4. Melt coconut oil in the same pan over medium-high heat. When oil is hot, working in batches so you don't crowd the pan, add shrimp and cook, turning once, until browned and just cooked through. Remove to a plate.

5. Serve cabbage, avocado, green onions, cilantro, jalapeño, and lime wedges in separate bowls. Have each person dress their own taco and drizzle with reserved marinade.

1 lb (450 g) medium raw shrimp (31/35), peeled and deveined

FOR THE MARINADE
½ cup (125 mL) coconut milk
¼ cup (60 mL) fresh cilantro leaves
1 Tbsp (15 mL) chopped chipotle pepper in adobo sauce
1 Tbsp (15 mL) olive oil
½ tsp (2 mL) minced garlic
½ tsp (2 mL) sea salt
Juice of ½ lime

FOR THE TACOS
12 corn tortillas
1 Tbsp (15 mL) coconut oil
¼ green cabbage, thinly sliced
2 avocados, thinly sliced
2 green onions, thinly sliced
1 cup (250 mL) fresh cilantro leaves
1 jalapeño pepper, thinly sliced
2 limes, cut in wedges

Pad Thai with Shrimp

This is a lighter but no less flavorful version of the classic you would get at a restaurant. The key to cooking this recipe is to set yourself up like a professional chef—have all your ingredients prepped and ready to go before you start cooking. Once you start cooking, everything will come together quickly. Note there isn't much sugar in this recipe. Soaking the noodles in naturally sweet coconut water makes more sweetness unnecessary.

···························· { DAIRY-FREE • GLUTEN-FREE } ····························

FOR THE NOODLES

8 oz (225 g) thin brown rice noodles (less than ¼ inch/ 5 mm wide)

2 cups (500 mL) unsweetened coconut water

2 cups (500 mL) hot water

FOR THE SAUCE

⅓ cup (75 mL) tamarind chutney

2 Tbsp (30 mL) fish sauce (gluten-free, if required)

1 Tbsp (15 mL) soy sauce (gluten-free, if required)

1 tsp (5 mL) coconut sugar

FOR THE TOPPING

¼ cup (60 mL) unsweetened desiccated coconut

¼ cup (60 mL) chopped salted roasted peanuts

Pinch of sea salt

FOR THE NOODLE MIXTURE

2 Tbsp (30 mL) coconut oil

3 cloves garlic, sliced

1 red chili, halved lengthwise, veins and seeds removed, and thinly sliced

2 eggs, lightly beaten

About 12 medium shrimp (31/35), peeled and deveined

6 green onions, cut in 1-inch (2.5 cm) pieces

2 large handfuls of bean sprouts

TO SERVE

A big handful of fresh cilantro leaves

1 lime, cut in 6 wedges

1. **PREPARE THE NOODLES** In a medium bowl, combine noodles, coconut water, and hot water. Leave to soak for about 20 minutes. Drain noodles, reserving ¼ cup (60 mL) soaking liquid. Set noodles and liquid aside.

2. **MAKE THE SAUCE** In a small bowl, stir together tamarind chutney, fish sauce, soy sauce, and coconut sugar until well blended. Set aside.

3. **MAKE THE TOPPING** In a large frying pan over medium heat, combine coconut, peanuts, and salt. Cook, stirring, until coconut is golden brown. Remove to a small bowl and return pan to heat.

4. **MAKE THE NOODLE MIXTURE** Melt coconut oil in the pan. When hot, add garlic and chili; cook, stirring, until garlic is translucent. Pour eggs into pan and stir quickly, then stir in shrimp. Stir in reserved noodles and soaking liquid. Cook for about 1 minute, stirring occasionally.

5. Stir in green onions and bean sprouts. Continue to cook, stirring often, until noodles are soft and green onions are just cooked.

6. Transfer to a large serving plate and top with coconut topping and cilantro. Serve with lime wedges.

Spicy Spaghetti with Crab

SERVES 4

The subtle sweetness of coconut milk goes beautifully with the briny, sweet flavor of crab. The chili flakes make this dish quite hot, so don't hesitate to start with less and add more if you like.

······································{ DAIRY-FREE ∗ GLUTEN-FREE }····································

1. In a large pot of salted boiling water, cook pasta until almost al dente.

2. **MEANWHILE, MAKE THE SAUCE** In a large frying pan over medium heat, combine olive oil, garlic, chili flakes, and salt. Cook, stirring occasionally, until garlic is soft but not browned.

3. Pour in wine. Raise heat to medium-high and cook until wine is reduced by half, about 3 minutes. Remove from heat.

4. When pasta has about a minute left to cook, return sauce to medium heat. Drain pasta, reserving ¼ cup (60 mL) cooking liquid. Add pasta to sauce along with crab, coconut milk, and reserved pasta water. Simmer gently, stirring, for about 1 minute.

5. Remove pan from heat and stir in lemon juice, basil, and parsley. Season with freshly cracked pepper and stir in Parmesan, if desired.

1 lb (450 g) spaghetti
  (gluten-free, if required)

FOR THE SAUCE
2 Tbsp (30 mL) olive oil

6 cloves garlic, thinly sliced

1 tsp (5 mL) chili flakes

1 tsp (5 mL) salt

½ cup (125 mL) dry white wine

1 lb (450 g) crabmeat,
  thawed if frozen

⅓ cup (75 mL) coconut milk

TO FINISH
Juice of 1 lemon

½ cup (125 mL) coarsely
  chopped fresh basil

½ cup (125 mL) coarsely
  chopped fresh parsley

Freshly cracked pepper

A handful of finely grated
  Parmesan cheese (optional)

Crispy Thai Tilapia Fingers

SERVES 4

This easy recipe yields lots of flavor with minimal effort. It has many of the elements of a traditional Thai curry, but comes together much quicker. The coconut flour adds a touch of sweetness. Tilapia is a great fish to cook with. It doesn't break up when it's cooked, it is very low in fat, and it works with many different flavorings.

·······················{ DAIRY-FREE * GLUTEN-FREE }·······················

2 tilapia fillets (8 oz/225 g each), each cut in 4 to 6 fingers

¼ cup (60 mL) coconut oil

FOR THE COATING

¼ cup (60 mL) cornstarch

¼ cup (60 mL) fresh cilantro, finely chopped

3 Tbsp (45 mL) coconut flour

1 kaffir lime leaf, very thinly sliced (or the zest of ½ lime)

¼ tsp (1 mL) chili flakes

1 tsp (5 mL) sea salt

2 egg whites

1 tsp (5 mL) tamari soy sauce (gluten-free, if required)

1 tsp (5 mL) fish sauce (gluten-free, if required)

1. **MAKE THE COATING** In a shallow dish, combine cornstarch, cilantro, coconut flour, lime leaf, chili flakes, and salt. Stir until well mixed.

2. In a separate shallow dish, whisk together egg whites, tamari sauce, and fish sauce.

3. Dip each piece of fish in egg white mixture, letting excess drip off, then dredge in cornstarch mixture, pressing mixture onto fish until it is well coated.

4. In a large frying pan over medium-high heat, heat coconut oil until shimmering. Working in batches so you don't crowd the pan, lower fish fingers into hot oil and fry until golden brown and cooked through, about 3 minutes per side.

Red Curry Grilled Salmon Skewers

SERVES 4

I am usually not a fan of skewers. Things tend to not cook properly when they are jammed together on a stick. These green onion and salmon skewers are an exception. The green onions add great flavor to the fish and become tender and delicious when grilled. Serve with rice.

··················{ DAIRY-FREE * GLUTEN-FREE }··················

1. Soak 12 (6-inch/15 cm) wooden skewers in cold water for at least an hour (or use metal skewers).

2. **MAKE THE MARINADE** In a large bowl, combine lemongrass, garlic, coconut milk, fish sauce, curry paste, coconut sugar, and salt. Stir until well combined.

3. Stir in salmon. Cover and refrigerate for at least 1 hour or up to 2 hours.

4. Preheat grill to medium-high. Oil grill.

5. **ASSEMBLE THE SKEWERS** Thread alternating pieces of salmon and green onion onto skewers. Grill, turning occasionally, until salmon is cooked through, about 3 minutes per side. Remove to a serving plate, sprinkle with chili slices and cilantro, and serve with lime wedges.

FOR THE MARINADE

1 stalk lemongrass, cut in ¼-inch (5 mm) pieces

1 clove garlic, chopped

1 cup (250 mL) coconut milk

2 Tbsp (30 mL) fish sauce (gluten-free, if required)

2 Tbsp (30 mL) red curry paste (gluten-free, if required)

1 Tbsp (15 mL) coconut sugar

1 tsp (5 mL) sea salt

FOR THE SKEWERS

1 lb (450 g) skinless salmon fillet, cut in 1-inch (2.5 cm) pieces

6 green onions, cut in 1-inch (2.5 cm) pieces

TO SERVE

1 red chili, thinly sliced

Fresh cilantro leaves

1 lime, cut in wedges

Salmon Cakes

SERVES 4

This is an update of a childhood staple of mine. Fresh salmon turns
it into an adult version, and the coconut flour and cornstarch
make a crisp crust against a very tender cake. These would make a
lovely lunch or a satisfying dinner with a simple green salad.

···{ DAIRY-FREE • GLUTEN-FREE }···

1 lb (450 g) Yukon Gold
    potatoes (about 3 medium),
    peeled and cut in 1-inch
    (2.5 cm) cubes

1 skin-on wild salmon fillet
    (1 lb/450 g)

Zest and juice of ½ lemon

½ cup (125 mL) fresh parsley
    leaves, coarsely chopped

1 Tbsp (15 mL) Dijon mustard
    (gluten-free, if required)

1 tsp (5 mL) sea salt

½ tsp (2 mL) chili flakes

Freshly ground black pepper

⅓ cup (75 mL) coconut flour

1 Tbsp (15 mL) cornstarch

3 Tbsp (45 mL) coconut oil

1 lemon, cut in wedges,
    for garnish

1. Place potatoes in a large pot and cover with cold water.
   Add salt and bring to a boil, then reduce heat and simmer,
   partially covered, until potatoes are fork-tender, about
   15 minutes. Lift potatoes from water and set aside in a
   bowl to cool.

2. In the same water, gently simmer salmon until just cooked
   through, about 5 minutes. Remove from water and set
   aside to cool. When cool enough to handle, remove skin
   and discard.

3. Mash potatoes coarsely. Add lemon zest and juice, parsley,
   mustard, salt, chili flakes, and black pepper to taste.
   Mix thoroughly.

4. Break salmon into large flakes using 2 forks or your fingers.
   Gently fold into potato mixture.

5. On a large plate, stir together coconut flour and cornstarch.

6. Shape salmon mixture into patties about ½ inch (1 cm)
   thick and 2½ inches (6 cm) across. Press each side of each
   patty into coconut flour. Transfer to a plate, cover, and
   refrigerate for about an hour before frying.

7. Melt coconut oil in a large nonstick frying pan over
   medium-high heat. When oil is hot, working in batches
   if necessary, fry patties until golden, about 4 minutes per
   side. Drain on paper towels. Serve with lemon wedges.

Sesame-Crusted Salmon with Spinach and Sesame Sauce

SERVES 4

This is a very sophisticated take on a one-pan dinner. As a bonus, the sesame crust makes it impossible for the fish to stick to the pan.

···{ DAIRY-FREE ∘ GLUTEN-FREE }···

1. **MAKE THE SAUCE** In a small bowl, stir together coconut cream, tamari sauce, ginger, Sriracha sauce, coconut sugar, and sesame oil. Set aside in a small pitcher.

2. **PREPARE THE SALMON** Season both sides of salmon with sea salt, then very generously sprinkle flesh side with sesame seeds.

3. In a large nonstick frying pan, melt coconut oil over medium-high heat. When oil is shimmering, add salmon, sesame seed side down, and cook until sesame seeds are golden brown, about 4 minutes.

4. Flip salmon to skin side. Cover, reduce heat to medium, and cook until salmon is just cooked through, 5 to 7 minutes. Remove salmon to plates or a platter.

5. Return pan to heat. Stir in spinach and toss until just wilted, about 1 minute. Arrange spinach on plates or platter. Garnish with lime wedges and green onions. Pass the sauce separately for drizzling over the fish and spinach.

FOR THE SAUCE

3 Tbsp (45 mL) coconut cream (scooped from the top of an unshaken chilled can of coconut milk)

1 Tbsp (15 mL) tamari soy sauce (gluten-free, if required)

1 tsp (5 mL) grated fresh ginger

1 tsp (5 mL) Sriracha sauce

½ tsp (2 mL) coconut sugar

½ tsp (2 mL) toasted sesame oil

FOR THE SALMON

4 wild salmon fillets (5 oz/140 g each)

1 tsp (5 mL) sea salt

⅓ cup (75 mL) sesame seeds

2 Tbsp (30 mL) coconut oil

4 cups (1 L) loosely packed baby spinach

TO SERVE

1 lime, cut in wedges

2 green onions (white and green parts), thinly sliced

Shepherd's Pie

SERVES 4

The high vegetable quotient in this recipe means you can get away with a
lot less meat, making it much healthier than its common counterparts.
But don't worry—it is still comfort food at its finest. You will not believe how rich
and creamy the mashed potato topping is, even without butter or cream.

{ DAIRY-FREE • GLUTEN-FREE }

FOR THE MASH

3 medium Yukon Gold potatoes,
    peeled and quartered

2 cups (500 mL) large
    cauliflower florets

1 cup (250 mL) chicken stock
    (gluten-free, if required)

1 cup (250 mL) coconut milk

1 tsp (5 mL) sea salt

2 Tbsp (30 mL) fresh
    thyme leaves

FOR THE FILLING

3 carrots, peeled and cut in
    2-inch (5 cm) pieces

2 ribs celery, cut in 2-inch
    (5 cm) pieces

1 red onion, quartered

1 lb (450 g) lean ground beef

1 sprig fresh thyme

⅓ cup (75 mL) unsweetened
    coconut water

3 Tbsp (45 mL) Worcestershire
    sauce (gluten-free, if
    required)

2 Tbsp (30 mL) soy sauce
    (gluten-free, if required)

1 Tbsp (15 mL) hot sauce

Pinch of ground allspice

2 Tbsp (30 mL) brown rice flour

1. **MAKE THE MASH** In a medium saucepan, combine potatoes, cauliflower, chicken stock, coconut milk, and salt. Bring to a boil, then reduce heat, cover, and simmer until potatoes are fork-tender. Remove pot from heat and set aside.

2. **MEANWHILE, MAKE THE FILLING** In a food processor, combine carrots, celery, and onion; pulse until vegetables are finely chopped. Set aside.

3. Place ground beef and thyme sprig in a large pot and cook over medium-high heat, stirring often, until beef is browned. Pour off any excess fat, then stir in chopped vegetables and cook for about 3 minutes. (Rinse out bowl of food processor and set aside to use for potato mixture.)

4. Stir in coconut water, Worcestershire sauce, soy sauce, hot sauce, and allspice. Bring to a boil, then reduce heat to low, cover, and simmer until vegetables are fork-tender.

5. Remove from heat. Discard thyme sprig. Stir in brown rice flour.

6. Place rack in middle of oven and preheat broiler to high.

7. Transfer filling to an 8-inch (2 L) square baking dish (or divide among 4 large ramekins and arrange ramekins on a baking sheet).

8. Lift potatoes and cauliflower out of their cooking liquid (reserving the liquid) and transfer to the food processor; pulse to a chunky mash. With the motor running, slowly pour in just enough cooking liquid to get a creamy mash. Stir in thyme leaves.

9. Spoon mash over filling. Broil until top is browned, 5 to 7 minutes.

Creamy Indian-Spiced Lamb Stew

SERVES 4

Another classic use for coconut milk, this stew's flavor is bright but deep at the same time. It gets better as it sits, so make it the day before and serve it with rice or warm naan or pitas brushed with olive oil and sprinkled with chopped cilantro.

·····················{ DAIRY-FREE * GLUTEN-FREE }·····················

1. In a food processor, combine onion, garlic, ginger, chili, cilantro stems, and almonds. Pulse until very finely chopped.

2. In a large saucepan over medium-low heat, melt coconut oil. Add lamb in batches (it will not brown if you crowd the pan) and brown on all sides, removing to a plate as browned. Pour off excess fat. Stir in tomato paste and cook for about 1 minute.

3. Stir in onion mixture, cardamom, salt, and cumin. Cook, stirring often, until just sticking to the bottom of the pan, about 3 minutes.

4. Pour in water and add lamb to saucepan. Raise heat to high, bring to a boil, then reduce heat to low. Cover and simmer until lamb is very tender, about 1½ hours. Add more water, ¼ cup (60 mL) at a time, if stew becomes too dry.

5. Just before serving, stir in coconut milk and lemon juice; simmer just to heat through. Serve garnished with cilantro and chili slices.

1 large onion, quartered

4 cloves garlic, peeled

1-inch (2.5 cm) piece
   fresh ginger, peeled and
   coarsely chopped

1 red chili, halved lengthwise
   and seeds removed (test
   chili for hotness, and
   proceed accordingly)

A handful of fresh cilantro
   stems

¼ cup (60 mL) ground almonds

1 Tbsp (15 mL) coconut oil

1½ lb (675 g) lamb
   stewing meat

2 Tbsp (30 mL) tomato paste

5 green cardamom
   pods, crushed

2 tsp (10 mL) sea salt

1 tsp (5 mL) ground cumin

1 cup (250 mL) water

½ cup (125 mL) coconut milk

Juice of ½ lemon

TO SERVE

A handful of fresh
   cilantro leaves

1 red chili, thinly sliced

Coconut-Braised Whiskey Ribs

SERVES 4 TO 6

The smoky-spicy rub gives these ribs a very good approximation of the bark formed in Texas barbecue. And the coconut water and whiskey steam them to fall-off-the-bone perfection. You can finish the ribs on the grill or in the oven.

·······················{ DAIRY-FREE * GLUTEN-FREE }······················

FOR THE RUB

4 tsp (20 mL) cayenne pepper

1 Tbsp (15 mL) ground coriander

2 Tbsp (30 mL) sea salt

2 Tbsp (30 mL) coconut sugar

2 tsp (10 mL) ground cumin

2 tsp (10 mL) chili powder

1 tsp (5 mL) smoked paprika

1 tsp (5 mL) onion powder

FOR THE RIBS

2 racks pork baby back ribs, membrane on underside removed

3 cups (750 mL) unsweetened coconut water

½ cup (125 mL) whiskey

FOR THE GLAZE

¼ cup (60 mL) whiskey

2 Tbsp (30 mL) honey

1. Preheat oven to 275°F (140°C).

2. **MAKE THE RUB** In a small bowl, stir together cayenne, coriander, salt, coconut sugar, cumin, chili powder, paprika, and onion powder. Set aside ¼ cup (60 mL) for the glaze.

3. **PREPARE THE RIBS** Rub remaining rub evenly over both sides of ribs. Place ribs flesh side up in a large roasting pan.

4. Pour coconut water and then whiskey around ribs. Cover tightly with foil and bake for 2½ hours or until meat is pierced easily with a fork. Set aside until ready to grill. (You can braise the ribs the day before. Remove from liquid, wrap in plastic wrap, and refrigerate. Bring to room temperature before grilling.)

5. **MAKE THE GLAZE** Stir together reserved rub, whiskey, and honey.

6. Preheat grill to medium-low (or preheat oven to 375°F/190°C and line a baking sheet with parchment paper).

7. Grill ribs flesh side up for about 10 minutes (or bake, flesh side up, on prepared baking sheet). Flip and brush with reserved glaze; flip and glaze again. Continue flipping and glazing until glaze is used up.

8. Remove ribs to a plate, tent loosely with foil, and let rest for about 10 minutes before cutting and serving.

Coconut Pork in Lettuce Wraps

SERVES 4

Cooking ground pork in coconut milk may sound unusual, but the milk infuses the meat with flavor and tenderizes it at the same time. This dish is fast and easy—and also very tasty. Not to mention a virtuous way to enjoy pork. If you are feeling super-virtuous, try this recipe with ground chicken. Either way, kids love any opportunity to make their own plate, so serve the toppings in lots of little bowls.

{ DAIRY-FREE * GLUTEN-FREE }

1. In a medium saucepan, combine coconut milk, chili, ginger, and garlic. Bring to a boil.

2. Stir in pork. Reduce heat and simmer, stirring, until coconut milk is absorbed and pork starts to brown. Stir in fish sauce, soy sauce, and coconut sugar. Transfer to a serving bowl.

3. Heat a small frying pan over medium heat. Add shredded coconut and sesame seeds; cook, stirring often, until coconut and seeds are light golden brown, about 4 minutes. Scrape into a small serving bowl.

4. Place rice, lettuce leaves, cilantro, mint, and green onions in serving bowls. Have each person spoon about ¼ cup (60 mL) rice into a lettuce cup and top with some pork mixture, then dress as desired, finishing with coconut mixture.

½ cup (125 mL) coconut milk

1 red chili

1 Tbsp (15 mL) grated fresh ginger

1 Tbsp (15 mL) minced garlic

1 lb (450 g) ground pork

1 Tbsp (15 mL) fish sauce (gluten-free, if required)

1 Tbsp (15 mL) soy sauce (gluten-free, if required)

1 tsp (5 mL) coconut sugar

TO SERVE

2 Tbsp (30 mL) unsweetened shredded coconut

2 Tbsp (30 mL) sesame seeds

1½ cups (375 mL) boiled sticky rice

1 to 2 heads iceberg lettuce, leaves separated

Leaves from ½ bunch fresh cilantro, chopped

Leaves from ½ bunch fresh mint, torn

4 green onions (white and green parts), sliced ¼ inch (5 mm) thick

Spiced Roasted Chicken

SERVES 4 TO 6

A little bit sweet and a little bit spicy. This is tastier than a store-bought rotisserie chicken, and the coconut oil makes for the crispiest skin. (The drier you get the skin before rubbing it with coconut oil, the crispier it will be.) This recipe just might make you abandon your trusty roast chicken recipe!

·········· { DAIRY-FREE · GLUTEN-FREE } ··········

FOR THE RUB

1 Tbsp (15 mL) sea salt

1 Tbsp (15 mL) coconut sugar

1 tsp (5 mL) ground cumin

1 tsp (5 mL) sweet paprika

1 tsp (5 mL) cayenne pepper

Pinch of ground allspice

Freshly ground black pepper

FOR THE CHICKEN

1 medium onion, sliced ¼ inch
   (5 mm) thick

A handful of fresh rosemary,
   thyme, or sage sprigs

1 chicken (3½ to 4 lb/1.6 to
   1.8 kg), rinsed and patted
   very dry

2 Tbsp (30 mL) coconut oil

1 cup (250 mL) dry white wine

1. **MAKE THE RUB** In a small bowl, stir together salt, coconut sugar, cumin, paprika, cayenne, allspice, and black pepper to taste.

2. **PREPARE THE CHICKEN** Scatter onion slices and herb sprigs in a roasting pan. Place chicken on top. Rub chicken all over with coconut oil. Sprinkle with rub and let sit at room temperature for about half an hour.

3. Meanwhile, preheat oven to 450°F (230°C).

4. Roast chicken, without basting, for 18 minutes per pound. When you have about 10 minutes of cooking time left, pour wine into the pan. Continue roasting until a meat thermometer reads 165°F (75°C) when inserted in the thickest part of the thigh.

5. Transfer chicken to a cutting board and let rest for at least 15 minutes before carving. Spoon off any excess fat from roasting pan and serve chicken with onion and juices from bottom of pan.

Coconut Chicken Fingers

SERVES 2 ADULTS OR 4 KIDS

I did not test this recipe on any kids, but I do have it on good authority that they will love it. You can double or triple the recipe and freeze the breaded fingers. Cook from frozen—add about 6 minutes to the cooking time. I serve these juicy, flavorful chicken fingers with hot sauce, but you can make a very quick honey mustard by stirring together equal parts runny honey and mustard of your choice.

················{ DAIRY-FREE · GLUTEN-FREE }················

1. Preheat oven to 500°F (260°C). Line a baking sheet with parchment paper and rub the coconut oil evenly over parchment.

2. **MAKE THE MAYONNAISE MIXTURE** In a shallow dish, stir together mayonnaise, mustard, salt, and cayenne.

3. **MAKE THE COATING** In another shallow dish, stir together cornmeal, coconut, and sesame seeds. Stir in green onions.

4. Dip each chicken strip into mayonnaise mixture, removing excess with your fingers. (You can also brush the mixture onto the chicken if you don't like mess.) Drop each strip into coating mixture, pressing to coat on all sides. Arrange on prepared baking sheet and let sit for about 15 minutes to ensure coating will stick to chicken.

5. Bake for 6 minutes, then flip and bake for an additional 6 to 10 minutes or until golden brown and cooked through.

2 Tbsp (30 mL) coconut oil

1 lb (450 g) boneless, skinless chicken breasts (2 medium), cut in 1-inch (2.5 cm) strips crosswise

FOR THE MAYONNAISE MIXTURE

2 Tbsp (30 mL) mayonnaise or coconut milk

2 Tbsp (30 mL) Dijon mustard (gluten-free, if required)

1 tsp (5 mL) sea salt

½ tsp (2 mL) cayenne pepper

FOR THE COATING

½ cup (125 mL) fine cornmeal

¼ cup (60 mL) unsweetened shredded coconut

2 Tbsp (30 mL) sesame seeds

2 green onions (white and green parts), thinly sliced

Crispy Fried Chicken

SERVES 4

Yes, this recipe calls for skinless chicken. Trust me, you really won't miss the skin! I've made the recipe both ways and actually prefer this version. This recipe might just replace your go-to fried chicken. It's just as delicious as the classic, but much healthier. You might have to take the skin off yourself, as most grocery stores don't sell skinless bone-in chicken pieces. Some paper towel and a pair of kitchen shears will make an easy job of it.

···························· { DAIRY-FREE • GLUTEN-FREE } ····························

2 lb (900 g) skinless, bone-in chicken drumsticks and thighs

1 to 2 cups (250 to 500 mL) coconut oil

FOR THE DREDGE

½ cup (125 mL) cornstarch

2 Tbsp (30 mL) thyme leaves

1 tsp (5 mL) sea salt

FOR THE MARINADE

1 can (14 oz/400 mL) coconut milk

3 Tbsp (45 mL) soy sauce (gluten-free, if required)

2 tsp (10 mL) hot sauce

A few sprigs fresh thyme

1. **MAKE THE DREDGE** In a medium bowl, stir together cornstarch, thyme, and salt. Set aside ⅓ cup (75 mL) for second dredging.

2. **MAKE THE MARINADE** In a large bowl, stir together coconut milk, soy sauce, hot sauce, and thyme sprigs.

3. Dredge chicken in cornstarch mixture in the bowl, coating thoroughly, then drop it into marinade. Discard dredge. Cover chicken and refrigerate for at least 2 hours or up to 4 hours.

4. Preheat oven to 375°F (190°C) and line a baking sheet with parchment paper.

5. Remove chicken from marinade (discard marinade). Dredge chicken in reserved cornstarch mixture. Let sit for about 10 minutes before frying. (Reserve remaining cornstarch mixture for testing oil.)

6. In a deep, wide cast-iron pan or Dutch oven over medium-high heat, heat coconut oil until it reaches 325°F (160°C) on a deep-fat thermometer (a pinch of the dredge will bubble when you drop it in the oil). Turn heat down to medium.

7. Working in batches so you don't crowd the pan, fry chicken pieces, turning once, until golden, about 6 minutes per side.

8. Place chicken on baking sheet and bake until cooked through, about 15 minutes.

Sticky Coconut-Glazed Chicken Wings

SERVES 2 AS A MAIN COURSE OR 4 AS AN APPETIZER

Who doesn't love a slightly sticky, sweet and spicy chicken wing?
A few of these served with some plain brown rice and kimchi
coleslaw (page 171) make a great meal, and you can substitute drumsticks
and thighs if you prefer them over chicken wings for dinner.

···································{ DAIRY-FREE • GLUTEN-FREE }···································

1. **MAKE THE MARINADE** In a large bowl, stir together coconut water and soy sauce. Add chicken wings, stirring to coat. Cover and refrigerate for at least 1 hour or up to 4 hours.

2. **MAKE THE GLAZE** In a small bowl, combine tamari sauce, coconut sugar, coconut vinegar, and cayenne. Stir until well mixed.

3. Preheat oven to 400°F (200°C) (or preheat grill to medium-low and lightly oil grill).

4. Remove wings from marinade and roast on a parchment-lined baking sheet (or grill), flipping and basting wings with glaze about 4 times, until wings are cooked, 35 to 40 minutes. Let rest for about 10 minutes before serving.

1½ lb (675 g) chicken wings

FOR THE MARINADE
1½ cups (375 mL) unsweetened coconut water
¼ cup (60 mL) soy sauce (gluten-free, if required)

FOR THE GLAZE
¼ cup (60 mL) tamari soy sauce (gluten-free, if required)
2 Tbsp (30 mL) coconut sugar
1 tsp (5 mL) coconut vinegar
½ tsp (2 mL) cayenne pepper

Duck Breast with
Thai Red Curry Eggplant

SERVES 4

Duck is one of my absolute favorite meats. It has a lean richness that
pairs beautifully with this spicy, slightly sweet, and creamy sauce and the
almost melted texture of the eggplant. If you've never cooked duck,
I urge you to try it. It cooks quicker than chicken and has tons of flavor.

·····················{ DAIRY-FREE * GLUTEN-FREE }·····················

2 duck breasts

Lime wedges, to serve

FOR THE EGGPLANT

1 Tbsp (15 mL) coconut oil

4 Japanese eggplants, halved
lengthwise and sliced
1½ inches (4 cm) thick

½ red onion, sliced ¼ inch
(5 mm) thick

2 stalks lemongrass, halved
lengthwise and cut in
2-inch (5 cm) pieces

1 red chili, halved lengthwise

1 cup (250 mL) coconut milk

¼ cup (60 mL) water

8 kaffir lime leaves

1 Tbsp (15 mL) red curry paste
(gluten-free, if required)

1 Tbsp (15 mL) fish sauce
(gluten-free, if required)

1 Tbsp (15 mL) soy sauce
(gluten-free, if required)

1. Using a very sharp knife, score duck skin in a crosshatch
   pattern about ⅛ inch (3 mm) deep and ¼ inch (5 mm) apart.
   Try not to cut into the flesh.

2. Place duck skin side down in a large frying pan. Cook
   slowly over medium heat, pouring off fat every few minutes, until skin is deep golden brown, about 12 minutes.

3. Flip duck and cook flesh side until browned, 3 to 4 minutes.
   Remove duck to a cutting board and let rest for at least
   10 minutes before slicing.

4. **WHILE DUCK IS RESTING, PREPARE THE EGGPLANT** Wipe pan
   with paper towel. Place over medium-high heat and melt
   coconut oil. When oil is hot, add eggplant large flat side
   down. Cook, without stirring, until golden brown, about
   2 minutes.

5. Stir in onion, lemongrass, and chili; cook for about
   2 minutes more.

6. Stir in coconut milk, water, lime leaves, curry paste, fish
   sauce, and soy sauce. Cook, stirring, until sauce is thickened slightly, about 1 minute. Remove lemongrass pieces,
   if desired, or pick them out as you eat. Pour mixture onto
   a platter.

7. Thinly slice duck breast and arrange on top of sauce.
   Serve with lime wedges and coconut rice.

Vegetarian Mains

RECICES

Gnocchi with Browned Butternut Squash and Crispy Sage

SERVES 4 TO 6

Homemade gnocchi is a very different thing from what you buy at the grocery store. It is tender and light, and the potato flavor really comes through. These freeze beautifully, so make ahead—or make extra—to have on hand for a quick meal. Having said that, feel free to use store-bought gnocchi if you're running short on time.

···{ DAIRY-FREE ∗ GLUTEN-FREE }···

FOR THE GNOCCHI

1 lb (450 g) Yukon Gold potatoes (unpeeled)

1½ tsp (7 mL) sea salt

⅓ to ½ cup (75 to 125 mL) brown rice flour

2 Tbsp (30 mL) coconut flour

1 egg, lightly beaten

3 Tbsp (45 mL) extra-virgin olive oil

FOR THE SAUCE

2 Tbsp (30 mL) coconut oil

A handful of fresh sage leaves

1 lb (450 g) butternut squash cut in ½-inch (1 cm) cubes (about 2 cups/500 mL)

½ tsp (2 mL) sea salt

3 cloves garlic, thinly sliced

¼ tsp (1 mL) chili flakes

½ cup (125 mL) coconut milk

⅓ cup (75 mL) finely grated Parmesan cheese, plus some shaved for garnish (optional)

Juice of ½ lemon

1. **MAKE THE GNOCCHI** Place potatoes in a medium pot and add enough cold water to just cover them. Add 1 tsp (5 mL) of the salt. Bring to a boil, then reduce heat and simmer until the tip of a sharp knife can easily pierce a potato to the middle.

2. Drain potatoes and let cool for about 30 minutes (potatoes should still be quite hot, but cool enough to handle).

3. Rice potatoes with a potato ricer (or grate them on the small holes of a box grater) into a large bowl (potatoes can be riced or grated without peeling). Add brown rice flour, coconut flour, and remaining ½ tsp (2 mL) salt; stir with a wooden spoon just until mixed, about 10 seconds. Add egg and stir just until you have a smooth, thick dough.

4. Bring a large pot of liberally salted water to a boil over high heat.

5. Sprinkle countertop with a good dusting of brown rice flour and scoop a small handful of dough onto the flour. Knead dough until it is no longer sticky, about 20 seconds. Roll into a rope about 10 inches (25 cm) long and ¾ inch (2 cm) thick. The rope will be fragile. Gently set aside. Repeat with remaining dough.

continued . . .

6. Line up 2 ropes beside each other and cut into 1-inch (2.5 cm) pieces with a small knife. Continue with remaining ropes. (At this point, you can freeze the gnocchi. Place in a single layer on a well-floured baking sheet and freeze. Transfer to a freezer bag or sealable container and keep frozen for up to 2 months.)

7. **COOK THE GNOCCHI** Pour the olive oil onto a baking sheet. Working in small batches, cook gnocchi (fresh or from frozen) in a pot of boiling salted water until they float, then remove with a slotted spoon to the oiled baking sheet. (Let gnocchi cool if you are not going to use them immediately. Toss gently in the oil, then remove to a sealable container and refrigerate for up to 2 days.)

8. **MAKE THE SAUCE** Melt coconut oil in a large frying pan over medium-high heat. When hot, add sage leaves. Cook until they darken slightly and become crisp, about 2 minutes, then drain on paper towel. Sprinkle lightly with salt.

9. Add butternut squash to the pan and toss with the salt. Cook, stirring occasionally, until browned and cooked through, about 8 minutes.

10. Stir in garlic and chili flakes. Cook, stirring often, until garlic is lightly browned, about 2 minutes more.

11. Stir in coconut milk and simmer just to heat through. Gently stir in gnocchi, Parmesan (if using), and lemon juice. Simmer just until gnocchi are heated through.

12. Remove to a platter or plates and top with sage leaves and shaved Parmesan (if using).

Curried Chickpeas with Spinach

SERVES 4

On weeknights we like to eat vegetarian meals, and this curry recipe originated on one of those nights. It makes an excellent dinner in the colder months, as it is hearty, filling, and packed with flavor—and also very healthy. Serve with plain boiled rice or quinoa. Or, if you prefer, warmed flatbread would be great alongside this dish.

·····················{ DAIRY-FREE ∗ GLUTEN-FREE ∗ VEGAN }·····················

1. In a large pot, melt coconut oil over medium-low heat. Stir in onion, chili flakes, and salt. Cook, stirring occasionally, until onion is soft and lightly browned.

2. Stir in cinnamon stick, garam masala, mustard seeds, and ginger. Cook, stirring often, until fragrant, about 1 minute.

3. Pour in chickpeas, water, and tomato. Raise heat to high and bring to a boil. Reduce heat to low and simmer, partially covered, for 10 minutes.

4. Just before serving, stir in spinach and coconut milk. Simmer until heated through. Serve garnished with cilantro, chili slices, and lemon wedges.

1 Tbsp (15 mL) coconut oil

½ red onion, chopped

¼ tsp (1 mL) chili flakes

1 tsp (5 mL) sea salt

1 cinnamon stick

1 tsp (5 mL) garam masala

1 tsp (5 mL) black mustard seeds

½ tsp (2 mL) ground ginger

1 can (14 oz/398 mL) chickpeas, drained and rinsed

½ cup (125 mL) water

1 medium tomato, diced

2 cups (500 mL) packed baby spinach

¾ cup (175 mL) coconut milk

TO SERVE

2 handfuls of fresh cilantro leaves

1 red chili, thinly sliced

1 lemon, cut in wedges

Coconut Curried Carrots with Cashews

SERVES 2

I first tried this combination in a Sri Lankan restaurant, and this recipe is a pretty close match. South Indian dishes make good use of coconut milk to balance out the spiciness. The cashews make this a very filling vegetarian dinner served with coconut rice (page 192), jasmine rice, or warm flatbread to soak up the sauce.

···{ DAIRY-FREE * GLUTEN-FREE * VEGAN }·································

½ white onion, thinly sliced

½ cup (125 mL) raw cashews

2 tsp (10 mL) coconut oil

1 tsp (5 mL) sea salt

½ tsp (2 mL) fennel seeds

¼ tsp (1 mL) chili flakes

2 lb (900 g) carrots, peeled, quartered lengthwise, and cut in 2-inch (5 cm) pieces

½ cup (125 mL) water

12 fresh curry leaves

½ tsp (2 mL) turmeric

½ tsp (2 mL) ground coriander

½ tsp (2 mL) ground cumin

1 cup (250 mL) coconut milk or light coconut milk

TO SERVE

½ cup (125 mL) fresh cilantro leaves

1 lime, cut in wedges

1. In a large pot over medium to medium-high heat, combine onion, cashews, coconut oil, salt, fennel seeds, and chili flakes. Cook, stirring often, until onion is soft.

2. Stir in carrots, then pour in water. Raise heat to high and bring to a boil, then reduce heat and simmer until carrots are almost cooked through, 8 to 12 minutes.

3. Stir in curry leaves, turmeric, coriander, cumin, and coconut milk. Simmer for about 5 minutes more. Serve garnished with cilantro and lime wedges.

Pizza with Figs and Garlic Cream

SERVES 4 TO 6

The garlic cream is what makes this pizza special—rich and aromatic and loaded with mellow garlic flavor. You can easily play around with the toppings. The garlic cream goes beautifully with a tomato-topped pizza with lots of fresh basil torn over it after baking. Or prosciutto and artichoke, or roasted red pepper and red onion with spinach . . . The possibilities are endless. No one will miss the cheese!

························{ DAIRY-FREE ∗ GLUTEN-FREE ∗ VEGAN }························

1. Divide pizza dough into 4 balls and let come to room temperature, covered with plastic wrap or a damp kitchen towel.

2. Place racks in upper and lower thirds of oven, and preheat oven to 400°F (200°C). Liberally dust 2 baking sheets with flour (gluten-free all-purpose, if required).

3. **MAKE THE GARLIC CREAM** In a small saucepan over medium heat, combine garlic, olive oil, and salt. Cook, stirring occasionally, until garlic is soft and just turning golden brown at the edges.

4. Stir in coconut cream; simmer until thickened slightly, about 1 minute. Remove from heat and blend with an immersion blender until just combined but still chunky.

5. Liberally dust countertop with flour. Working with 1 ball of dough at a time, roll (or stretch by hand) into a circle about 10 inches (25 cm) across. Place on prepared baking sheet. Top each with one-quarter of the garlic cream, spreading evenly to within ½ inch (1 cm) of the edge. Top with remaining toppings.

6. Bake, switching baking sheets halfway, for about 15 minutes or until browned on the bottom. Broil each pizza in upper third of oven until crust is browned. Drizzle with honey (if using) once out of the oven.

1 lb (450 g) pizza dough (gluten-free, if required)

FOR THE GARLIC CREAM
6 large cloves garlic, sliced
2 Tbsp + 1½ tsp (37 mL) extra-virgin olive oil
½ tsp (2 mL) sea salt
½ cup (125 mL) coconut cream (spooned from the top of an unshaken chilled can of coconut milk)

FOR THE TOPPINGS
½ red onion, thinly sliced
Leaves from 4 sprigs fresh rosemary or thyme
12 fresh figs, halved or quartered, depending on size
1 cup (250 mL) walnut halves
Runny honey (optional)

Zucchini Mozzarella Fritters

SERVES 4

These fritters make a great vegetarian main course served with a salad and a bit of chutney for dipping. You can also make the fritters a bit smaller and serve them as an appetizer if you like. Make sure to use fresh mozzarella—the kind that comes in a container with water. It forms a beautiful golden crust when it hits the pan.

···{ GLUTEN-FREE }···

3 medium zucchini

1 tsp (5 mL) sea salt

1 egg, lightly beaten

¼ cup (60 mL) brown rice flour

¼ cup (60 mL) unsweetened desiccated coconut

1 Tbsp (15 mL) cornstarch

2 tsp (10 mL) baking soda

2 green onions (white and green parts), thinly sliced

½ cup (125 mL) basil leaves, torn (optional)

1 ball (4 oz/113 g) fresh mozzarella cheese, patted dry and cut in ½-inch (1 cm) cubes

¼ cup (60 mL) grated Parmesan cheese

Pinch of chili flakes

4 Tbsp (60 mL) coconut oil

1. Preheat oven to 350°F (180°C).

2. Grate zucchini on the large holes of a box grater, then place on a clean kitchen towel spread out on a large plate. Sprinkle ½ tsp (2 mL) of the salt evenly over zucchini and let sit for about 5 minutes.

3. Lift corners of towel around zucchini and, working over the sink, squeeze out as much water as possible.

4. In a large bowl, stir together egg, brown rice flour, coconut, cornstarch, and baking soda. Gently stir in green onions, basil (if using), mozzarella, Parmesan, chili flakes, and remaining ½ tsp (2 mL) salt.

5. Melt about 2 Tbsp (30 mL) of the coconut oil in a medium nonstick frying pan over medium-high heat. When oil starts to shimmer, working in batches to avoid crowding the pan, add zucchini mixture by heaping spoonfuls. Fry, turning once, until golden brown, about 2 minutes per side. Drain on paper towel. Add more oil to pan between batches if necessary.

6. Fritters can be reheated in a single layer on a baking sheet for about 10 minutes before serving.

Pasta with Toasted Walnuts and Herb Pesto

SERVES 4

This is a very easy pasta dish, as there is not much fussing with pans and timing. The coconut milk makes the pesto gratifyingly creamy and very subtly sweet. You can prepare the pesto in advance, if you prefer, then stir it into the hot pasta. The pesto is also delicious drizzled over thickly sliced ripe tomatoes.

··{ DAIRY-FREE * GLUTEN-FREE * VEGAN }··

1. Bring a large pot of salted water to a boil. Cook pasta until almost al dente.

2. **MEANWHILE, MAKE THE PESTO** In a tall container, combine arugula, parsley, basil, garlic, lemon zest, salt, chili flakes, and coconut milk. Blend with an immersion blender until herbs are finely chopped.

3. When pasta is almost al dente, in a small frying pan over medium-high heat, combine walnuts, parsley, coconut oil, and salt. Cook, stirring often, until walnuts are toasted and parsley is crisp.

4. Drain pasta, return it to the pot, and toss with the pesto. Stir in walnuts and parsley, season with pepper, and serve immediately.

1 lb (450 g) pasta (gluten-free or vegan, if required)

1 cup (250 mL) walnut pieces

½ cup (125 mL) fresh parsley leaves

1 Tbsp (15 mL) coconut oil

¼ tsp (1 mL) sea salt

Freshly ground pepper

FOR THE PESTO

2 cups (500 mL) arugula

½ cup (125 mL) fresh parsley leaves

¼ cup (60 mL) fresh basil leaves

1 clove garlic, finely chopped

Zest of 1 lemon

½ tsp (2 mL) sea salt

¼ tsp (1 mL) chili flakes

½ cup (125 mL) coconut milk

Creamy Pasta with Peas and Basil

SERVES 4 TO 6

Pasta is one of my favorite choices for easy weeknight meals. I find it filling, comforting, and very quick to prepare. There are loads of gluten-free and alternative-flour pastas in grocery stores these days, and they really are almost indistinguishable from their wheaty counterparts, particularly when you combine them with a flavorful sauce such as this one. The lemon and basil are a fresh and bright foil for the richness and depth of the coconut milk and garlic.

························· { GLUTEN-FREE ∗ VEGAN } ·························

1 lb (450 g) penne or rigatoni (gluten-free or vegan, if required)

2 Tbsp (30 mL) extra-virgin olive oil

5 large cloves garlic, sliced

1 tsp (5 mL) sea salt

¼ cup (60 mL) dry white wine

½ cup (125 mL) coconut milk

2 cups (500 mL) green peas, thawed if frozen

1 cup (250 mL) fresh basil leaves, torn or coarsely chopped

⅓ cup (75 mL) grated Parmesan cheese (optional) or 1 tsp (5 mL) tamari soy sauce (gluten-free, if required)

2 Tbsp (30 mL) lemon juice

Freshly ground pepper

1. Bring a large pot of salted water to a boil. Cook pasta until almost al dente.

2. Meanwhile, in a large frying pan over medium heat, cook olive oil, garlic, and salt, stirring often, until garlic is soft and just beginning to turn golden brown at the edges.

3. Pour in wine; cook until pan is almost dry, about 1 minute. Stir in coconut milk and peas; simmer for about 3 minutes.

4. Drain pasta and add to coconut milk mixture. Simmer, stirring occasionally, until pasta is al dente, about 1 minute.

5. Stir through basil, Parmesan (if using), and lemon juice. Serve immediately, sprinkled with freshly ground pepper.

Mushroom Tart with Caramelized Onion Cream

SERVES 4

The crispy, golden phyllo crust is a great contrast to the deep, sweet flavor of the caramelized onion cream and mushrooms. The caramelized onion cream on its own is a delicious sauce to serve with simple roasted pork or chicken.

···{ DAIRY-FREE • VEGAN }···

1. **MAKE THE ONION CREAM** In a large frying pan over medium-high heat, combine onion, garlic, coconut oil, salt, and vinegar. Cook, stirring occasionally, until onion is soft and golden brown, about 10 minutes. Let onions cool slightly.

2. Transfer about half the onions to a tall container. Add coconut milk. Using an immersion blender, blend until smooth. Set aside onions and onion cream.

3. Preheat oven to 400°F (200°C).

4. **PREPARE THE TART SHELL** Brush some of the coconut oil on a baking sheet, then lay 1 sheet of phyllo on the baking sheet. (Keep remaining phyllo covered with a barely damp kitchen towel so it does not dry out.) Brush phyllo with coconut oil. Top with another sheet and brush with oil. Repeat with remaining phyllo. Trim to fit your baking sheet if necessary.

5. Spread onion cream evenly over phyllo, leaving a ½-inch (1 cm) border. Top with reserved caramelized onions. Top with zucchini, green onions, and mushrooms.

6. Bake for 15 to 20 minutes or until phyllo is golden and crisp.

7. Meanwhile, toss together arugula, chives, lemon juice, and olive oil. Scatter arugula over tart and serve immediately.

FOR THE ONION CREAM
1 white onion, thinly sliced
4 cloves garlic, sliced
1 Tbsp (15 mL) coconut oil
½ tsp (2 mL) salt
½ tsp (2 mL) red or
    white wine vinegar
½ cup (125 mL) coconut milk

FOR THE TART SHELL
¼ cup (60 mL) coconut
    oil, melted
10 sheets phyllo pastry, thawed

FOR THE TOPPINGS
1 small zucchini, shaved in
    strips with a vegetable
    peeler
4 green onions (or 1 small red
    onion), thinly sliced
¼ lb (115 g) mushrooms, sliced
    or torn in small pieces

TO FINISH
2 cups (500 mL) arugula
½ bunch fresh chives, snipped
Juice of ½ lemon
Extra-virgin olive oil

Vegetarian Chili with Coconut and Charred Eggplant

SERVES 4

Coconut adds good chew to this wholesome chili, something that is often missing from vegetarian chili, I find. The charred eggplant adds a smoky flavor and a great texture to this recipe. This is a spicy, rich-tasting vegan chili that everyone will enjoy.

·················· { DAIRY-FREE * GLUTEN-FREE * VEGAN } ··················

FOR THE EGGPLANT

1 medium to large eggplant, cut in ½-inch (1 cm) pieces (about 3 cups/750 mL)

1 Tbsp (15 mL) extra-virgin olive oil

½ tsp (2 mL) sea salt

FOR THE CHILI

1 white onion, chopped

1 small sweet red pepper, diced

3 cloves garlic, chopped

¼ cup (60 mL) fresh cilantro

stems, finely chopped

1 tsp (5 mL) sea salt

1 tsp (5 mL) coconut oil

1 Tbsp (15 mL) chili powder, or to taste

1 tsp (5 mL) ground cumin

2 cans (14 oz/398 mL each) black beans, drained and rinsed

1 can (28 oz/796 mL) diced tomatoes

¾ cup (175 mL) corn kernels (optional)

½ cup (125 mL) unsweetened shredded coconut

2 Tbsp (30 mL) chopped pickled jalapeño peppers (optional)

TO SERVE

Avocado slices

½ cup (125 mL) fresh cilantro leaves

2 green onions (white and green parts), thinly sliced

1 lime, cut in wedges

1. Preheat oven to 475°F (240°C) and generously rub a baking sheet with coconut oil.

2. **PREPARE THE EGGPLANT** Spread eggplant in a single layer on prepared baking sheet. Sprinkle with olive oil and salt. Roast for about 10 minutes or until browning. Stir, then roast for 10 more minutes or until soft and dark brown.

3. Transfer eggplant to a cutting board and let sit until cool enough to handle. Finely chop eggplant.

4. **MAKE THE CHILI** In a large pot over medium-high heat, combine onion, red pepper, garlic, cilantro, salt, and coconut oil. Cook, stirring often, until onion is soft, about 5 minutes. Stir in chili powder and cumin; cook, stirring, for about 1 minute.

5. Stir in eggplant, black beans, tomatoes, corn (if using), coconut, and pickled jalapeño (if using). Bring to a boil, then reduce heat to low and simmer for about 20 minutes. Serve topped with avocado, cilantro, green onions, and lime wedges.

Crunchy Coconut Falafels

MAKES ABOUT 24 BALLS

I love falafels, so had to include a recipe in this book. The authentic texture depends entirely on starting with dried chickpeas. I tried using canned chickpeas, but they just don't work. Coconut oil is the very best frying oil. It yields the ideal falafel—fluffy on the inside and crisp on the outside. These falafels make a great vegetarian main course alongside Middle Eastern chopped salad (page 79) and eggplant dip (page 54).

{ DAIRY-FREE * GLUTEN-FREE * VEGAN }

1. In a medium bowl, combine chickpeas, water, and baking soda. Let soak for at least 8 hours.

2. Drain chickpeas. In a food processor, combine chickpeas, onion, garlic, parsley, cilantro, coconut, salt, cumin, coriander, and chili flakes. Process until chickpeas are coarsely chopped.

3. Add chickpea flour, baking powder, and lemon juice. Pulse until incorporated. Let mixture rest for at least 15 minutes or up to 1 hour.

4. Form a heaping tablespoon of falafel mixture into a ball by squeezing mixture between your palms. Flatten into a patty. Dip each side into sesame seeds (if using). Repeat with remaining falafel mixture.

5. In a large frying pan over medium-high heat, melt coconut oil. Fry patties in batches, turning once, until golden brown, about 3 minutes per side. Drain on paper towel. Serve with pickles and olives.

1 cup (250 mL) dried chickpeas

3 cups (750 mL) water

¼ tsp (1 mL) baking soda

½ white onion, cut in large chunks

2 cloves garlic

¼ cup (60 mL) fresh parsley leaves

¼ cup (60 mL) fresh cilantro leaves

¼ cup (60 mL) unsweetened desiccated coconut

1¼ tsp (6 mL) sea salt

1 tsp (5 mL) ground cumin

½ tsp (2 mL) ground coriander

¼ tsp (1 mL) chili flakes

½ cup (125 mL) chickpea flour

½ tsp (2 mL) baking powder

Juice of ½ lemon

¼ cup (60 mL) sesame seeds (optional)

¼ cup (60 mL) coconut oil

Huevos Rancheros with Coconut Cilantro Cream

SERVES 4 TO 6

This twist on the classic works equally well as a brunch or dinner. It may look like a complicated recipe, but the main components just get chucked into a pot or jar and blended. Really simple. The black bean dip makes a great appetizer served with tortilla chips, and the zesty cilantro cream is excellent as a sauce for grilled fish or shrimp.

····················· { DAIRY-FREE · GLUTEN-FREE } ·····················

FOR THE BLACK BEANS

1 can (14 oz/398 mL) black beans, drained and rinsed

1 small clove garlic, minced

⅓ cup (75 mL) coconut milk

¼ cup (60 mL) water

1 Tbsp (15 mL) finely chopped pickled jalapeño pepper

½ tsp (2 mL) ground cumin

½ tsp (2 mL) chili powder

½ tsp (2 mL) sea salt

¼ cup (60 mL) fresh cilantro, coarsely chopped

1 green onion (white and green part), thinly sliced

1 Tbsp (15 mL) lime juice

FOR THE CILANTRO CREAM

½ cup (125 mL) fresh cilantro leaves

½ cup (125 mL) coconut milk

1 small clove garlic, coarsely chopped

2 Tbsp (30 mL) coarsely chopped pickled jalapeño pepper

1 tsp (5 mL) lime juice

½ tsp (2 mL) sea salt

¼ tsp (1 mL) ground cumin

FOR THE TORTILLAS AND EGGS

2 Tbsp (30 mL) coconut oil

4 to 6 corn tortillas

4 to 6 eggs

TO SERVE

Fresh cilantro leaves

Good store-bought salsa

Sliced avocado

Lime wedges

1. **PREPARE THE BLACK BEANS** In a medium saucepan, combine black beans, garlic, coconut milk, water, jalapeño, cumin, chili powder, and salt. Bring to a boil, then reduce heat and simmer, stirring occasionally, until sauce has thickened, 7 to 10 minutes.

2. Remove from heat and blend with an immersion blender until slightly chunky. Set aside.

3. **MAKE THE CILANTRO CREAM** In a tall container, combine cilantro, coconut milk, garlic, jalapeño, lime juice, salt, and cumin. Blend with an immersion blender until well mixed. Set aside.

4. Preheat oven to 250°F (120°C).

5. **PREPARE THE TORTILLAS AND EGGS** In a large nonstick frying pan over medium-high heat, melt 1 Tbsp (15 mL) of the coconut oil. Fry 1 corn tortilla at a time until soft. Remove to a plate and keep warm in the oven.

6. In the same pan over medium heat, melt remaining 1 Tbsp (15 mL) coconut oil. When hot, fry eggs just until whites are set.

7. Meanwhile, stir cilantro, green onion, and lime juice into black bean mixture.

8. To serve, divide bean mixture among tortillas, then top each serving with an egg. Drizzle with cilantro cream and garnish with cilantro, salsa, avocado, and lime wedges.

Sides

RECIPES

Roasted Cauliflower and Cashews

SERVES 4

This dish takes its method from Italian cooking while retaining a very Indian flavor. Just mix everything together and toss it in the oven. Curry leaves play a big part in this dish; look for them in Asian markets. If you can't find them, substitute a teaspoon (5 mL) of whole fennel seeds for an aromatic hit. Freeze leftover leaves in a freezer bag for up to three months.

························· { DAIRY-FREE · GLUTEN-FREE · VEGAN } ·····························

1 small head cauliflower, cut into small florets

12 fresh curry leaves

½ cup (125 mL) raw cashews

⅔ cup (150 mL) coconut milk

1 Tbsp (15 mL) black mustard seeds

1½ tsp (7 mL) sea salt

1 tsp (5 mL) ground cumin

½ tsp (2 mL) chili flakes

1. Preheat oven to 450°F (230°C) and line a baking sheet with parchment paper.

2. In a large bowl, combine cauliflower, curry leaves, cashews, coconut milk, mustard seeds, salt, cumin, and chili flakes. Toss until well mixed.

3. Spread out on prepared baking sheet and roast, stirring occasionally, until cauliflower is lightly browned and just tender, about 35 minutes.

Coleslaw with Kimchi

SERVES 6

Kimchi packs a punch, and using it allows you to whip up a flavor-packed coleslaw. The coconut milk is a healthier alternative to mayonnaise here, and the kimchi is loaded with probiotic goodies for your gut health. If you want this recipe to be vegan, check the list of ingredients in your kimchi; some contain fish.

·····················{ DAIRY-FREE * GLUTEN-FREE * VEGAN (OPTION) }·····················

1. **MAKE THE DRESSING** In a large bowl, combine coconut cream, lime juice, ketchup, tamari sauce, coconut sugar, Sriracha sauce, and sesame oil. Stir well.

2. **MAKE THE COLESLAW** Add kale, apple, and kimchi to dressing. Mix until well coated. (Coleslaw can be refrigerated for a few hours at this point.)

3. Just before serving, sprinkle with green onions, cilantro, and sesame seeds.

FOR THE DRESSING

⅓ cup (75 mL) coconut cream (scooped from the top of an unshaken chilled can of coconut milk)

1 Tbsp (15 mL) lime juice

2 tsp (10 mL) ketchup (gluten-free, if required)

2 tsp (10 mL) tamari soy sauce (gluten-free, if required)

1 tsp (5 mL) coconut sugar

½ to 1 tsp (2 to 5 mL) Sriracha sauce

½ tsp (2 mL) sesame oil

FOR THE COLESLAW

1 bunch kale, shredded (about 4 cups/1 L), or ¼ head cabbage, shredded, or a mix

1 red apple, cored and thinly sliced

½ cup (125 mL) kimchi (vegan, if required)

TO SERVE

2 green onions (white and green parts), sliced

½ cup (125 mL) fresh cilantro leaves

¼ cup (60 mL) sesame seeds, lightly toasted

Roasted Brussels Sprouts with Bacon

SERVES 6

Coconut may sound like an unusual ingredient in this recipe, but it really works to extend the crisp, slightly sweet smokiness of the very little bit of bacon used. And in fact you could leave the bacon out entirely for a vegan side dish. If desired, add ½ tsp (2 mL) smoked paprika for a hit of smoke to round out the sweetness of the coconut and dates.

···················{ DAIRY-FREE · GLUTEN-FREE · VEGAN (OPTION) }···················

1 Tbsp (15 mL) coconut oil

3 slices bacon, cut in ¼-inch (5 mm) strips

1 lb (450 g) Brussels sprouts, halved lengthwise

½ cup (125 mL) unsweetened coconut water

⅓ cup (75 mL) chopped pitted dates

¼ cup (60 mL) unsweetened flaked coconut

½ tsp (2 mL) sea salt

Pinch of chili flakes (optional)

TO SERVE

Juice of ½ lemon

A handful of fresh parsley leaves

Freshly cracked black pepper

1. Rub a baking sheet with the coconut oil. Scatter bacon on the baking sheet, put the bacon in the oven, and set the oven to 450°F (230°C) so the bacon will begin to cook as the oven heats up.

2. Meanwhile, in a large bowl, toss together Brussels sprouts, coconut water, dates, coconut, salt, and chili flakes (if using).

3. When bacon is almost crisp, pour Brussels sprouts mixture onto the hot baking sheet. Roast, stirring a few times, until sprouts are lightly browned and tender-crisp, 16 to 20 minutes.

4. Finish with a squeeze of lemon and transfer to a serving dish. Scatter with parsley and season with pepper.

Crispy Kale with Hazelnut Dressing

SERVES 4

I love that kale has become such a ubiquitous vegetable recently. It bodes well for our collective health. The slightly sweet and nutty dressing is a delicious contrast to the crispy bittersweetness of the charred kale. Any kind of kale works in this dish.

························{ DAIRY-FREE · GLUTEN-FREE · VEGAN }························

1. Preheat oven to 450°F (230°C).

2. **PREPARE THE KALE** Grease a baking sheet with the coconut oil and arrange kale pieces on sheet in a single layer. Scatter half of the hazelnuts over the kale and sprinkle with salt. Roast for 10 to 12 minutes, checking frequently and turning once, until the edges of the kale leaves are brown and crispy.

3. **MEANWHILE, MAKE THE DRESSING** In a small bowl, combine apple, hazelnuts, coconut cream, lemon juice, honey, salt, and cayenne. Stir to combine well.

4. Arrange kale and remaining hazelnuts on a platter. Drizzle with dressing and serve immediately to preserve the crispness of the kale.

FOR THE KALE
2 Tbsp (30 mL) coconut oil

1 large bunch kale, stems removed, leaves torn in large pieces, dried well

¼ cup (60 mL) coarsely chopped hazelnuts

½ tsp (2 mL) sea salt

FOR THE DRESSING
½ Granny Smith apple, chopped

¼ cup (60 mL) coarsely chopped hazelnuts

¼ cup (60 mL) coconut cream (spooned from the top of an unshaken chilled can of coconut milk)

2 Tbsp (30 mL) lemon juice

1 tsp (5 mL) honey

¼ tsp (1 mL) sea salt, or more to taste

⅛ tsp (0.5 mL) cayenne pepper

Cheddar Jalapeño Biscuits

MAKES 8 TO 10 BISCUITS

These biscuits are best served warm with a side of chili (page 158).
They are pretty quick to make, and the less you mix the batter the lighter
and more tender they will be. The rest in the fridge is key: it makes the
biscuits bake up higher and lighter than they otherwise would.

....{ GLUTEN-FREE }..

1½ cups (375 mL) brown
   rice flour

2 Tbsp (30 mL) coconut flour

1½ tsp (7 mL) baking powder

1 tsp (5 mL) baking soda

½ tsp (2 mL) sea salt

2 cups (500 mL) shredded
   old Cheddar

¼ cup (60 mL) chopped pickled
   jalapeño peppers

1 green onion (white and green
   part), thinly sliced

¾ cup (175 mL) coconut milk,
   plus more for brushing

1. In a large bowl, stir together brown rice flour, coconut flour, baking powder, baking soda, and salt. Stir in cheese, then stir in jalapeño and green onion, mixing well.

2. Using your fingers, work coconut milk through flour mixture until it forms a shaggy dough that holds together when you squeeze a handful. This should take about 20 seconds.

3. Lightly dust countertop with brown rice flour. Turn dough out onto countertop and knead just until it holds together, about 10 seconds. Do not overmix. Gather dough into a ball, flatten into a disk, then wrap in plastic wrap and refrigerate for at least 1 hour.

4. Preheat oven to 350°F (180°C) and line a baking sheet with parchment paper.

5. Lightly dust counter with brown rice flour. Pat dough into an 8-inch (20 cm) square. Using a 2-inch (5 cm) cutter, cut out 8 to 10 rounds. Flip each biscuit, then place at least 1 inch (2.5 cm) apart on prepared baking sheet. Brush tops with a little coconut milk.

6. Bake until golden, about 20 minutes. Serve warm.

Crispy Herb and Garlic Fries

SERVES 4

This is lazy cooking at its best, delivering lots of flavor for little effort! You don't do much more than crush the garlic and scatter the herbs around the potatoes to really perfume the whole dish—in fact, your whole kitchen.

·······················{ DAIRY-FREE * GLUTEN-FREE * VEGAN }·······················

1. Preheat oven to 300°F (150°C) and line a baking sheet with parchment paper. Grease parchment with the coconut oil.

2. Spread potatoes, garlic, and thyme sprigs on baking sheet. Sprinkle with salt.

3. Place pan in oven and increase temperature to 400°F (200°C). Roast until potatoes are golden brown on the bottom, about 15 minutes. Flip potatoes and cook for 15 to 20 minutes more, until golden brown all over. Serve immediately.

3 Tbsp (45 mL) coconut oil

3 large russet or baking potatoes, each cut in 8 wedges

4 cloves garlic (unpeeled), smashed

4 sprigs fresh thyme or rosemary

1 tsp (5 mL) sea salt

Creamy Sweet Potato Mash with Crispy Shallots and Sage

SERVES 4 TO 6

This dish is sure to become a regular at holiday dinners. Warm and comforting, it goes well with almost any roast you can think to make. I bet no one will notice the absence of cream and butter—here replaced by coconut milk. It is important, for the texture of the mash, to use a ricer or masher. A food processor or electric mixer results in an undesirably gluey mash.

·····························{ DAIRY-FREE * GLUTEN-FREE }·····························

FOR THE POTATOES

1 lb (450 g) Yukon Gold potatoes, peeled and quartered

1 large sweet potato, peeled and cut in 8 pieces

1 cup (250 mL) chicken stock (gluten-free, if required)

1 cup (250 mL) coconut milk

1 tsp (5 mL) sea salt

FOR THE SHALLOTS AND SAGE

1 Tbsp (15 mL) coconut oil

Leaves from ½ bunch fresh sage (about ½ cup/125 mL loosely packed)

¼ tsp (1 mL) sea salt

1 large shallot, peeled and thinly sliced

1. **PREPARE THE POTATOES** In a large saucepan, combine Yukon Gold potatoes, sweet potato, chicken stock, coconut milk, and salt. Bring to a boil over high heat, then reduce heat to low, cover, and simmer until potatoes are fork-tender, about 25 minutes.

2. **MEANWHILE, PREPARE THE SHALLOTS AND SAGE** In a small frying pan, heat coconut oil over medium-high heat until it shimmers. Working in batches if necessary, place sage leaves in a single layer in hot oil. Cook, turning once, until leaves are dark and crisp, about 2 minutes.

3. Drain sage on paper towel. Sprinkle with a little salt.

4. In the same pan, cook shallot until golden brown, stirring often, about 3 minutes. Remove from heat and set aside.

5. Drain potatoes, reserving about ½ cup (125 mL) cooking liquid, and return potatoes to pot. Mash with a masher or put through a food mill or ricer. Stir in some cooking liquid until you have a creamy mixture.

6. Transfer mash to a serving bowl. Scrape shallots with their oil over mash. Top with sage leaves.

Squash Gratin

SERVES 4 TO 6

I love any root vegetable layered and cooked in cream. Coconut milk makes this a far healthier version, but it's no less satisfying than traditional scalloped potatoes. You can substitute an onion for the leeks if you like, or leave them out altogether and increase the amount of squash a bit.

·························{ DAIRY-FREE · GLUTEN-FREE }··························

1. Preheat oven to 400°F (200°C) and grease a casserole dish with coconut oil.

2. **PREPARE THE SQUASH** In a large frying pan over medium-high heat, cook leeks, garlic, coconut oil, and salt, stirring occasionally, until leeks are almost soft.

3. Pour in wine and chicken stock. Simmer until reduced by half, about 5 minutes. Stir in coconut milk and remove from heat.

4. Spread about half of the leek mixture in the casserole dish. Top with about half of the squash slices. Season with salt and pepper. Repeat, ending with squash.

5. Cover tightly with foil and bake until squash slices are easily pierced with the tip of a knife, 25 to 30 minutes.

6. **MEANWHILE, MAKE THE TOPPING** In a small bowl, stir together bacon, bread crumbs, Parmesan (if using), rosemary, and chili flakes.

7. Uncover casserole and sprinkle topping mixture evenly over squash. Continue to bake until bread crumbs are browned and bacon is bubbling, about 15 minutes. Let sit for at least 10 minutes before serving.

FOR THE SQUASH

2 leeks (white and light green parts), halved lengthwise and sliced ¼ inch (5 mm) thick

2 cloves garlic, smashed

2 tsp (10 mL) coconut oil

½ tsp (2 mL) sea salt

½ cup (125 mL) dry white wine

½ cup (125 mL) chicken stock (gluten-free, if required)

¾ cup (175 mL) coconut milk

1 butternut squash, peeled, halved lengthwise, seeds and pulp removed, sliced ⅛ inch (3 mm) thick

Freshly ground pepper

FOR THE TOPPING

2 slices bacon, finely chopped

½ cup (125 mL) dry bread crumbs (gluten-free, if required)

⅓ cup (75 mL) grated Parmesan cheese (optional)

1 Tbsp (15 mL) chopped fresh rosemary

½ tsp (2 mL) chili flakes

Tomato Gratin

SERVES 4

This recipe can bring out the best in the lowliest mid-winter grocery-store tomato. It's best made, however, when tomatoes are at the peak of ripe perfection. It's important to let the gratin sit for a few minutes after it comes out of the oven, so the sauce can thicken slightly. Feel free to leave out the Parmesan cheese if you want a vegan version.

·······················{ DAIRY-FREE · GLUTEN-FREE · VEGAN (OPTION) }·······················

1½ lb (675 g) assorted tomatoes, sliced ¼ inch (5 mm) thick or halved (if cherry)

FOR THE GARLIC CREAM
4 large cloves garlic, sliced
1 Tbsp (15 mL) extra-virgin olive oil
1 Tbsp (15 mL) coconut oil
½ tsp (2 mL) sea salt
½ cup (125 mL) coconut milk

FOR THE TOPPING
¼ cup (60 mL) dry bread crumbs (gluten-free, if required)
¼ cup (60 mL) finely grated Parmesan cheese (optional)
2 Tbsp (30 mL) fresh thyme leaves
1 Tbsp (15 mL) extra-virgin olive oil

1. Place rack in middle of oven and preheat oven to 400°F (200°C).

2. **MAKE THE GARLIC CREAM** In a small saucepan over medium-high heat, combine garlic, olive oil, coconut oil, and salt. Cook until garlic just begins to brown. Pour in coconut milk and simmer for 3 minutes or until mixture thickens slightly. Set aside.

3. **MAKE THE TOPPING** In a small bowl, stir together bread crumbs, Parmesan (if using), thyme, and olive oil. Set aside.

4. Arrange tomatoes in a shallow layer in a large pie plate or shallow baking dish. Pour garlic cream over tomatoes and sprinkle with topping mixture.

5. Bake for 10 minutes, then broil until topping is golden brown, about 5 minutes. Let sit for 5 to 10 minutes before serving.

Chili-Garlic Roasted Green Beans

SERVES 4

Inspired by a Chinese takeout staple, salty, spicy, and with a bit of sweetness in the charred bits, this recipe makes beans exciting! Roasting is a great way to concentrate the flavors of vegetables without losing all their vitamins to a pot of water.

{ DAIRY-FREE * GLUTEN-FREE * VEGAN }

1. Preheat oven to 450°F (230°C) and grease a baking sheet with the coconut oil.

2. Spread beans in a single layer on the baking sheet and roast for 8 minutes, stirring once after 4 minutes.

3. While beans are roasting, in a small bowl, combine tamari sauce, cornstarch, garlic, and chili flakes. Stir until well mixed.

4. When beans are almost tender-crisp, pour soy sauce mixture over them. Roast for 2 minutes more or until beans are cooked to your liking.

2 Tbsp (30 mL) coconut oil
¾ lb (340 g) French green beans, trimmed
2 Tbsp (30 mL) tamari soy sauce (gluten-free, if required)
1 tsp (5 mL) cornstarch
1 clove garlic, finely chopped
¼ tsp (1 mL) chili flakes

Creamy White Beans
with Crispy Prosciutto

SERVES 4

It really doesn't matter whether you use cannellini, borlotti, or white navy beans in this dish. I tend to use cannellini, simply because I always seem to have a few cans in my pantry. This comforting dish makes a nice change from mashed potatoes and has loads more fiber. The prosciutto is optional, but it adds lots of flavor for such a small amount.

························{ DAIRY-FREE * GLUTEN-FREE * VEGAN (OPTION) }························

2 leeks (white and light green parts), halved lengthwise and sliced ¼ inch (5 mm) thick

2 large cloves garlic, sliced

1 Tbsp (15 mL) coconut oil

1½ tsp (7 mL) sea salt

¼ cup (60 mL) dry white wine

4 sprigs fresh thyme

1 can (14 oz/398 mL) cannellini beans, drained and rinsed

½ cup (125 mL) coconut milk

2 thin slices prosciutto (optional)

1. In a large frying pan over medium-high heat, combine leeks, garlic, coconut oil, and sea salt. Cook, stirring often, until leeks are soft but not browned.

2. Pour wine over leeks and stir in thyme sprigs. Simmer until pan is almost dry, about 3 minutes.

3. Stir in beans and coconut milk. Simmer until coconut milk thickens slightly, about 4 minutes.

4. Meanwhile, if using prosciutto, heat a small nonstick frying pan over medium heat. When it is hot, cook prosciutto in dry pan, turning once, until crisp, about 3 minutes. Remove from pan.

5. Remove thyme sprigs from beans. Pour beans into a serving bowl and crumble prosciutto over top.

Creamy Corn Pudding

SERVES 4

This pudding captures the essence of corn flavor with bright and spicy hits from the Mexican pantry. The coconut milk is a natural and absolutely delicious pairing with the corn, and adds a luscious creaminess without any cream. You can use frozen corn in a pinch, but this pudding is best made when fresh corn is at its peak. It is best served with pork chops or a simple roasted chicken.

·······················{ DAIRY-FREE * GLUTEN-FREE * VEGAN }·····················

1. Place rack in middle of oven and preheat broiler.

2. In a large frying pan over medium-high heat, combine onion, coconut oil, and salt. Cook, stirring often, until onion is soft.

3. Stir in corn; cook until soft, about 5 minutes.

4. Reduce heat to medium-low and stir in coconut milk, cornmeal, and jalapeño. Simmer gently until mixture thickens, about 4 minutes.

5. Remove from heat and stir in cilantro. Pour mixture into a casserole dish. Broil until top is browned, about 8 minutes. Garnish with cilantro leaves and jalapeño slices.

½ white onion, finely chopped

1 Tbsp (15 mL) coconut oil

1 tsp (5 mL) sea salt

3 ears corn, kernels removed (about 3 cups/750 mL)

1 cup (250 mL) coconut milk

2 Tbsp (30 mL) fine cornmeal

1 Tbsp (15 mL) finely chopped pickled jalapeño pepper

½ cup (125 mL) fresh cilantro leaves

TO SERVE

Fresh cilantro leaves

Sliced pickled jalapeño peppers

Coconut Rice

SERVES 4

Here is a coconut classic. The sesame seeds and green onions are optional but add nuttiness and punch to nicely balance the slightly sweet and rich rice. This is perfect served with any Indian or Asian dish, or as a side dish for any sort of roasted meat. The towel under the lid absorbs steam so the rice will not get gluey.

···················· { DAIRY-FREE * GLUTEN-FREE * VEGAN } ····················

1½ cups (375 mL) long-grain rice (preferably basmati or jasmine)

1½ cups (375 mL) water

½ cup (125 mL) coconut milk

½ tsp (2 mL) sea salt

TO SERVE (OPTIONAL)

¼ cup (60 mL) sesame seeds, lightly toasted

2 green onions (white and green parts), thinly sliced

1. In a medium saucepan, combine rice, water, coconut milk, and salt; stir well. Bring to a boil over high heat, then reduce heat to low, cover, and simmer until rice is tender but not mushy and liquid is absorbed, about 15 minutes.

2. When rice is cooked, remove pot from heat. Uncover and drape a kitchen towel over the pot. Cover with the lid and let rice rest for a few minutes before serving.

3. Serve rice in a large bowl, garnished with sesame seeds and green onions, if desired.

Desserts

RECITPES

Baklava Florentines

This makes a fairly small batch of cookies, but they should be eaten quite soon after baking. On a humid day they will very likely go a bit soft and sticky, but they will still taste good.

·························{ DAIRY-FREE * GLUTEN-FREE }····························

1. Preheat oven to 325°F (160°C) and line 2 baking sheets with parchment paper.

2. In a large bowl, stir together egg white, icing sugar, cinnamon, baking soda, and salt. Gently stir in coconut, almonds, walnuts, pistachios, and lemon zest until evenly coated.

3. Drop by the heaping tablespoon onto prepared baking sheets. Bake 1 sheet at a time until golden brown on the bottom and firm to the touch, about 12 minutes.

4. Let cool on baking sheets for about 3 minutes before removing to a rack to cool completely. Store in an airtight container.

1 egg white

⅓ cup (75 mL) icing sugar (gluten-free, if required)

½ tsp (2 mL) cinnamon

½ tsp (2 mL) baking soda

¼ tsp (1 mL) sea salt

⅔ cup (150 mL) unsweetened shredded coconut

⅔ cup (150 mL) sliced almonds

⅓ cup (75 mL) chopped walnuts

¼ cup (60 mL) chopped pistachios

½ tsp (2 mL) very finely grated lemon zest

Peanut Butter Coconut Cookies

Besides being delicious and really quick to make, these cookies are high in fiber and relatively low in sugar. The coconut gives them a satisfying chew and a pleasing toasty flavor. You can substitute other nut butters if you like, and use milk chocolate instead to make these more kid-friendly.

·······················{ DAIRY-FREE · GLUTEN-FREE }·······················

¼ cup (60 mL) coconut oil

1 cup (250 mL) unsweetened flaked coconut

1½ cups (375 mL) peanut butter

½ cup (125 mL) white sugar

¼ cup (60 mL) coconut sugar

2 eggs, lightly beaten

2 Tbsp (30 mL) brown rice flour

¼ tsp (1 mL) sea salt

3½ oz (100 g) dark chocolate, cut in chunks

1. Preheat oven to 325°F (160°C) and line a baking sheet with parchment paper.

2. Combine coconut oil and coconut in a small frying pan over medium heat. Cook, stirring often, until coconut is light golden brown. Set aside to cool for at least 10 minutes.

3. In a large bowl, combine peanut butter, white sugar, coconut sugar, eggs, brown rice flour, and salt; stir until completely combined. Add coconut mixture; mix well.

4. Drop by the tablespoon onto prepared baking sheet. Press a chunk of chocolate onto each cookie. Bake until cookies are golden on the bottom, 10 to 14 minutes.

5. Let cool on baking sheet for a few minutes before transferring to a rack to cool completely. Store in an airtight container.

Coconut Almond Chocolate Macaroons

MAKES ABOUT 20 MACAROONS

These are pretty enough to bring to a party but healthy enough to eat for breakfast. Use a good-quality dark chocolate. You can replace the whole almonds with dried cherries for a delicious alternative.

{ DAIRY-FREE * GLUTEN-FREE * VEGAN }

1. In a food processor, combine coconut, almond flour, coconut oil, agave syrup, almond extract, and salt. Process until mixture starts to come together into a ball around the processor blade.

2. Line a plate with parchment paper. Roll about a tablespoon (15 mL) of macaroon mixture into a 1-inch (2.5 cm) ball and press onto the plate. Press an almond (if using) into the top of each macaroon.

3. Place chocolate (if using) in a small microwave-safe bowl and cook on Medium, stirring every 20 seconds, until melted.

4. Dip each macaroon into the chocolate (or drizzle chocolate over macaroons). Let sit at room temperature until chocolate has hardened, about 1 hour.

1½ cups (375 mL) unsweetened shredded coconut
½ cup (125 mL) almond flour
2 Tbsp (30 mL) coconut oil
2 Tbsp (30 mL) agave syrup
1 tsp (5 mL) almond extract
⅛ tsp (0.5 mL) sea salt
20 raw almonds (optional)
2 oz (55 g) dark chocolate, chopped (for optional drizzle), or 4 oz (115 g) dark chocolate, chopped (for optional dipping)

Double Chocolate Nut Brownies

These brownies are rich, dense, and fudgy, which is a great thing for chocolate brownies, in my opinion. They can be divided into large squares and served warm with a scoop of vanilla ice cream for dessert, or cut into 16 and eaten as a snack.

...................................{ DAIRY-FREE · GLUTEN-FREE }....................................

1. Preheat oven to 350°F (180°C) and line an 8-inch (20 cm) square cake pan with a 12- × 8-inch (30 × 20 cm) strip of parchment paper, leaving two "handles" to lift the baked brownies out of the pan.

2. In a medium saucepan over medium-low heat (or in a medium microwaveable bowl), melt chocolate and coconut oil, stirring occasionally. Set aside to cool for about 10 minutes.

3. In a medium bowl, stir together cornstarch, cocoa, and salt until well blended.

4. In a large bowl, stir together eggs, coconut milk, coconut sugar, white sugar, and vanilla until well mixed.

5. Stir cornstarch mixture into egg mixture, then stir in melted chocolate until well blended. Fold in nuts. Pour batter into prepared pan. Smooth top of brownies.

6. Bake until a toothpick inserted in the center of brownies comes out almost clean, 35 to 45 minutes. Let cool in pan for at least 10 minutes, then lift out of pan and cool on a rack for about an hour before cutting. Store in an airtight container.

2 cups (500 mL) good-quality semisweet chocolate chips

¼ cup (60 mL) coconut oil

6 Tbsp (90 mL) cornstarch

¼ cup (60 mL) cocoa powder

½ tsp (2 mL) sea salt

3 eggs, lightly beaten

6 Tbsp (90 mL) coconut milk

¼ cup (60 mL) coconut sugar

¼ cup (60 mL) white sugar

1 tsp (5 mL) vanilla extract

1 cup (250 mL) chopped pecans or walnuts

Sesame Ice Cream

There is a very slight bitterness in tahini that makes this a really interesting ice cream. You can substitute ⅓ cup (75 mL) peanut butter for the tahini and sesame oil if you wanted to make this for kids.

·························· { DAIRY-FREE * GLUTEN-FREE * VEGAN } ··························

1 can (14 oz/400 mL)
    coconut milk

1 cup (250 mL) unsweetened
    rice milk

⅓ cup (75 mL) maple syrup or
    honey

4 tsp (20 mL) tahini

1 Tbsp (15 mL) vanilla extract

1 tsp (5 mL) toasted sesame oil

¼ tsp (1 mL) sea salt

TO SERVE

2 pkg (1¼ oz/35 g each)
    sesame brittle snacks,
    crushed

1. In a tall container, combine coconut milk, rice milk, maple syrup, tahini, vanilla, sesame oil, and salt. Blend with an immersion blender until smooth. Refrigerate mixture for at least 2 hours.

2. Process in an ice-cream maker according to the manufacturer's directions. Transfer ice cream to a container and freeze for at least 4 hours.

3. Let ice cream soften at room temperature for about 10 minutes before serving. Divide among bowls and top each serving with crushed sesame snacks.

Strawberry Ice Cream

MAKES 1 QUART (1 L)

This ice cream tastes like the height of summer. Fresh local strawberries have the best flavor, of course, but you can use frozen strawberries in a pinch. The xanthan gum is optional, but it does make ice cream made without cream or eggs more custardy, and indeed you'll see it starting to work the minute you mix it in.

························{ DAIRY-FREE ∗ GLUTEN-FREE ∗ VEGAN }························

1. In a large bowl, combine coconut milk, strawberries, icing sugar, agave syrup, salt, xanthan gum (if using), and lime juice. Stir until thoroughly combined. Refrigerate mixture for at least 4 hours.

2. Process in an ice-cream maker according to the manufacturer's directions. Transfer ice cream to a container and freeze for at least 4 hours.

3. Let ice cream soften at room temperature for about 10 minutes before serving.

3 cups (750 mL) coconut milk

1½ cups (375 mL) mashed strawberries (2 cups/ 500 mL whole)

2 Tbsp (30 mL) icing sugar (gluten-free, if required)

2 Tbsp (30 mL) agave syrup

½ tsp (2 mL) sea salt

¼ tsp (1 mL) xanthan gum (optional)

Juice of ½ lime

Coconut Dulce de Leche

We dip almost anything into this versatile sauce, but raw or grilled pineapple is especially nice. Or spoon some over ice cream. You can easily double this recipe. Just cook it for a little longer, and remember, when it chills it will thicken up quite a bit.

{ DAIRY-FREE · GLUTEN-FREE · VEGAN }

1 can (14 oz/400 mL) coconut milk
⅓ cup (75 mL) coconut sugar
⅓ cup (75 mL) white sugar
¼ tsp (1 mL) sea salt

1. In a medium saucepan, combine coconut milk, coconut sugar, white sugar, and salt. Bring to a boil, then reduce heat to low and simmer, stirring occasionally, until mixture darkens and goes quite thick, 20 to 30 minutes. It will thicken further as it is chilled.

2. Transfer to a jar and refrigerate until cold. Sauce keeps, refrigerated, for up to a week.

Maple Rice Pudding

Maple syrup and coconut milk are a sublime match, and the almonds add a depth of flavor and texture that most rice puddings lack. My favorite way to eat this dessert is slightly warm, with cold coconut milk and maple syrup drizzled on top. It makes a very good winter weekend breakfast.

·····················{ DAIRY-FREE * GLUTEN-FREE * VEGAN }·····················

1. Set aside ¼ cup (60 mL) of the coconut milk for serving.

2. In a medium saucepan, combine rice, coconut, ground almonds, salt, cinnamon, coconut water, and remaining coconut milk. Bring to a boil, then reduce heat to low, cover, and simmer, stirring occasionally, until rice is tender, 25 to 30 minutes. If rice looks dry, add some more water, ¼ cup (60 mL) at a time.

3. Remove from heat and stir in maple syrup and vanilla. Let sit for about 10 minutes.

4. Spoon into bowls and top with reserved coconut milk, sliced almonds, and a drizzle of maple syrup.

1 can (14 oz/400 mL) coconut milk

1 cup (250 mL) short-grain white rice

¼ cup (60 mL) unsweetened desiccated coconut

¼ cup (60 mL) ground almonds (preferably freshly ground)

¼ tsp (1 mL) sea salt

2 cinnamon sticks (or ½ tsp/ 2 mL cinnamon)

1½ cups (375 mL) unsweetened coconut water

¼ cup (60 mL) maple syrup

1 tsp (5 mL) vanilla extract

TO SERVE
A handful of sliced almonds
A drizzle of maple syrup

Chocolate Pudding

This pudding doesn't contain cornstarch thickener, so there is no constant stirring and trying to decide if the mixture is coating the back of a spoon. No pitfalls, just good, old-fashioned pudding! The peanut butter adds just a hint of peanut butter flavor. You can leave it out entirely or increase to ½ cup (125 mL) if you prefer.

······························{ GLUTEN-FREE }······························

1 can (14 oz/400 mL) coconut milk

5 oz (140 g) semisweet chocolate, chopped

1 oz (28 g) white chocolate, chopped

¼ cup (60 mL) peanut butter (optional)

1 tsp (5 mL) vanilla extract

¼ tsp (1 mL) sea salt

TO SERVE

1 oz (28 g) semisweet chocolate, shaved

1. In a medium saucepan over medium heat, bring coconut milk just to a boil. Remove from heat and immediately stir in semisweet chocolate, white chocolate, peanut butter (if using), vanilla, and salt. Stir until chocolate is melted and mixture is smooth.

2. Divide pudding among dessert dishes and refrigerate, uncovered, until set, at least 2 hours. Serve garnished with shaved chocolate.

Peach Custard with Burnt Almonds

SERVES 4

This quick dessert is best made with peaches that aren't overly ripe. The baking coaxes a sweetness and softness from them. Apricots work well here, too, and if they are small, slice up one per person to top each custard.

························{ DAIRY-FREE * GLUTEN-FREE }························

1. Place rack in middle of oven and preheat oven to 275°F (140°C). Grease 4 shallow 1-cup (250 mL) ramekins with coconut oil.

2. In a medium saucepan, bring coconut milk to a boil. Remove from heat. Whisk 2 Tbsp (30 mL) of the hot milk into the egg yolks, then stir mixture back into the pot.

3. Stir in almond flour, maple syrup, almond extract, and salt until combined.

4. Divide mixture among ramekins and top each with 8 peach slices. Sprinkle with sliced almonds and then evenly sprinkle with sugar.

5. Bake for 10 minutes, then broil on middle rack until almonds are slightly toasted and sugar is slightly melted, about 3 minutes. Do not overcook. Serve drizzled with a little coconut milk.

1½ cups (375 mL) coconut milk, plus extra for serving

2 egg yolks, lightly beaten

2 Tbsp (30 mL) almond flour

2 Tbsp (30 mL) maple syrup

½ tsp (2 mL) almond extract

¼ tsp (1 mL) sea salt

2 firm-ripe peaches, each pitted and cut in 16 slices

½ cup (125 mL) sliced almonds

2 Tbsp (30 mL) evaporated cane sugar or white sugar

Cranberry Sticky Toffee Pudding

SERVES 8

This is a rich, cozy winter dessert that's best served warm (reheat puddings in muffin tins so they don't dry out) and drizzled with warm sauce. The cranberries should be fresh or frozen, not dried. You want that hit of sourness against all the sweet richness of the dates and the creamy sauce. The pudding should be served soon after it's topped with the sauce. If you plan to make the pudding ahead and reheat it before serving, make the sauce and top the pudding just before serving.

···{ DAIRY-FREE • GLUTEN-FREE }···

FOR THE PUDDING

1¼ cups (300 mL) pitted dates, coarsely chopped

¾ cup (175 mL) water

½ cup (125 mL) coconut sugar

¼ cup (60 mL) unsweetened shredded coconut

3 Tbsp (45 mL) coconut oil

2 tsp (10 mL) baking soda

½ cup (125 mL) brown rice flour

¼ cup (60 mL) coconut flour

1½ tsp (7 mL) baking powder

½ tsp (2 mL) ground ginger

3 eggs, lightly beaten

¾ cup (175 mL) fresh or thawed frozen cranberries, coarsely chopped

FOR THE SAUCE

½ cup (125 mL) lightly packed coconut sugar

¼ cup (60 mL) white sugar

½ cup (125 mL) orange juice

⅓ cup (75 mL) coconut milk

2 Tbsp (30 mL) coconut oil

1. **MAKE THE PUDDING** Place dates, water, coconut sugar, and coconut in a medium saucepan. Cover and bring to a boil, stirring occasionally. Reduce heat and simmer, stirring occasionally, until dates are very soft, about 3 minutes. Remove from heat and stir in coconut oil until melted. Stir in baking soda. Let cool.

2. Preheat oven to 325°F (160°C) and grease (with coconut oil) and flour (with brown rice flour) 8 cups of a muffin pan.

3. In a medium bowl, stir together brown rice flour, coconut flour, baking powder, and ginger.

4. Gradually stir in date mixture just until combined. Stir in eggs, then stir in cranberries.

5. Spoon batter into prepared muffin cups, filling almost to the rim and distributing cranberries evenly. Place pan in oven, reduce heat to 300°F (150°C), and bake until a tester inserted in the center of pudding comes out almost clean, 30 to 35 minutes.

6. Let rest on a rack for 10 minutes. Run a knife around each pudding to loosen and gently turn out puddings.

7. **WHILE PUDDINGS REST, MAKE THE SAUCE** In a medium saucepan, combine coconut sugar, white sugar, orange juice, coconut milk, and coconut oil. Bring to a boil over medium-high heat and boil gently, stirring occasionally, until slightly thickened, 5 to 6 minutes.

8. Serve puddings warm topped with warm sauce, or pass sauce separately.

Blueberry Apple Crumble

SERVES 4 TO 6

This crumble is sweet and toasty, with just a touch of tartness from the berries and apples. It is much better made ahead and reheated before serving. The syrup around the fruit will be very juicy when it comes out of the oven but will thicken up as it sits. Kids love rubbing the crumble ingredients together, if you'd like to outsource that part of the job.

. . . . { DAIRY-FREE • GLUTEN-FREE • VEGAN } . . . .

1. Preheat oven to 350°F (180°C).

2. **PREPARE THE FRUIT** In a large bowl, stir together apples, blueberries, coconut sugar, cornstarch, vanilla, and lemon zest. Turn into an 8-inch (20 cm) square baking dish.

3. **MAKE THE CRUMBLE** In a medium bowl, combine almonds, walnuts, coconut, coconut sugar, almond flour, cornstarch, cinnamon, ginger, and salt. Add coconut oil and rub mixture between your fingers until oil is well distributed and the mixture is crumbly, about 30 seconds.

4. Sprinkle topping evenly over fruit. Bake until topping is golden brown and fruit is bubbly, about 45 minutes. Let sit for at least 45 minutes before serving.

FOR THE FRUIT

3 Golden Delicious apples, peeled, cored, and coarsely chopped

4 cups (1 L) frozen wild blueberries

3 Tbsp (45 mL) coconut sugar

2 Tbsp (30 mL) cornstarch

1 tsp (5 mL) vanilla extract

Zest of 1 lemon

FOR THE CRUMBLE

½ cup (125 mL) sliced almonds

½ cup (125 mL) chopped walnuts

6 Tbsp (90 mL) unsweetened shredded coconut

⅓ cup (75 mL) coconut sugar

¼ cup (60 mL) almond flour

2 Tbsp (30 mL) cornstarch

½ tsp (2 mL) cinnamon

¼ tsp (1 mL) ground ginger

¼ tsp (1 mL) sea salt

¼ cup (60 mL) coconut oil

Coconut Cream Pie

There was no question that this recipe absolutely had to be in this book. After I made it, every time I went into the kitchen, the pie was a little bit smaller, which is the very best compliment. The white chocolate is the secret ingredient here. It adds a deep sweet flavor that goes beautifully with coconut. This pie is big enough to serve 8 to 10 quite easily, especially if you top it with the vanilla whipped coconut milk (page 17). If you are using the pie shell for a savory filling, omit the coconut sugar.

···{ DAIRY-FREE ∗ GLUTEN-FREE }···

FOR THE PIE SHELL

1½ cups (375 mL) almond flour

1 cup (250 mL) brown rice flour

¼ cup (60 mL) coconut oil

2 Tbsp (30 mL) coconut flour

2 tsp (10 mL) coconut sugar

½ tsp (2 mL) sea salt

2 egg whites

FOR THE FILLING

¼ cup (60 mL) cornstarch

¼ tsp (1 mL) salt

1 can (14 oz/400 mL) coconut milk

1 cup (250 mL) milk of your choice

2 egg yolks

3 oz (85 g) white chocolate, finely chopped

1 cup (250 mL) unsweetened flaked coconut

¼ cup (60 mL) agave syrup

2 tsp (10 mL) vanilla extract

1 tsp (5 mL) coconut extract (optional)

1. **MAKE THE PIE SHELL** In a food processor, combine almond flour, brown rice flour, coconut oil, coconut flour, coconut sugar, salt, and egg whites. Process just until combined.

2. Pour mixture into a 9-inch (23 cm) springform pan and, using your fingers or the bottom of a drinking glass, press evenly over the bottom and halfway up the sides the pan. Poke crust all over with a fork.

3. Bake for 25 minutes or until light golden brown. Set aside to cool.

4. **MAKE THE FILLING** Combine cornstarch and salt in a medium saucepan. Slowly whisk in coconut milk and milk. Cook over medium heat just until mixture starts to bubble, about 3 minutes.

5. Whisk 2 Tbsp (30 mL) of the milk mixture into the egg yolks, then stir mixture back into pot. Cook, stirring constantly, until mixture starts to thicken, about 3 minutes more.

6. Remove from heat and whisk in white chocolate, coconut, agave syrup, vanilla, and coconut extract (if using) until chocolate is melted and filling is smooth.

7. Pour into pie shell and refrigerate until fully set, at least 2 hours.

8. Just before serving, if desired, beat coconut cream and icing sugar with an electric mixer until soft peaks form. Top each serving with cream and toasted flaked coconut.

TO SERVE

½ cup (125 mL) coconut cream (scooped from the top of an unshaken chilled can of coconut milk; optional)

1 Tbsp (15 mL) icing sugar (gluten-free, if required; optional)

⅓ cup (75 mL) unsweetened flaked coconut, toasted in a nonstick pan over medium heat until golden brown

Carrot Cake

SERVES 8 TO 10

Red lentils are, I realize, a strange thing to put in a cake, but I was determined to bake this cake on a day when I didn't have enough carrots on hand. My search for all things orange accounts for the sweet potato, too. The happy result is a surprisingly delicious cake, which tastes even better the next day. The frosting recipe makes enough to frost the top and middle of the cake; double the recipe if you want to frost the sides as well.

·······················{ DAIRY-FREE * GLUTEN-FREE }·······················

1. Preheat oven to 325°F (160°C). Grease (with coconut oil) and flour (with brown rice flour) two 8-inch (20 cm) round cake pans.

2. **MAKE THE CAKE** In a small saucepan, bring lentils, coconut milk, and water to a boil. Stir, reduce heat, and cover. Simmer, stirring occasionally, until lentils are tender, about 15 minutes. Let cool for about 10 minutes, then stir in baking soda.

3. In a small frying pan over medium heat, melt coconut oil with shredded coconut. Cook, stirring often, until coconut starts to brown. Let cool slightly.

4. In a large bowl, combine brown rice flour, almond flour, coconut flour, baking powder, salt, cinnamon, nutmeg, and walnuts. Stir until well combined.

5. In a medium bowl, whisk together eggs, coconut sugar, and maple syrup. Stir in carrots, lentils, toasted coconut, sweet potato, and apple. Add to dry ingredients and stir just until combined.

6. Pour into prepared pans and bake until cakes are not jiggly in the middle and a toothpick inserted in the center just comes out clean, 30 to 35 minutes. Do not overbake!

continued ...

FOR THE CAKE

¼ cup (60 mL) red lentils

⅔ cup (150 mL) coconut milk

¼ cup (60 mL) water

¼ tsp (1 mL) baking soda

⅓ cup (75 mL) coconut oil

⅓ cup (75 mL) unsweetened shredded coconut

1¼ cups (300 mL) brown rice flour

½ cup (125 mL) almond flour

2 Tbsp (30 mL) coconut flour

2 tsp (10 mL) baking powder

½ tsp (2 mL) sea salt

½ tsp (2 mL) cinnamon

¼ tsp (1 mL) nutmeg

½ cup (125 mL) chopped walnuts

4 eggs

½ cup (125 mL) coconut sugar

½ cup (125 mL) maple syrup

2 large carrots, peeled and grated

½ medium sweet potato, peeled and grated

1 apple, peeled and grated

7. Let cool in pans for about 10 minutes. Turn cakes out onto racks to cool completely before frosting.

8. **MAKE THE FROSTING** In a large bowl, using an electric mixer, beat coconut oil with ¼ cup (60 mL) of the icing sugar, vanilla, and salt until creamy.

9. Stop mixer. Add maple syrup, 2 Tbsp (30 mL) of the coconut milk, and 2 cups (500 mL) icing sugar. Stir on low speed until fully combined, then beat on medium-high speed for about 1 minute. Scrape down sides of bowl. Add more icing sugar, ¼ cup (60 mL) at a time, if icing is too thin. Add the remaining coconut milk if icing is too stiff. Beat until frosting is creamy, about 1 minute more.

10. Place 1 cake layer on a cake plate and spread with half of the frosting. Top with second cake layer and spread top with remaining frosting.

FOR THE FROSTING
2 Tbsp (30 mL) coconut oil
2 to 3 cups (500 to 750 mL) icing sugar (gluten-free, if required)
1 tsp (5 mL) vanilla
¼ tsp (1 mL) sea salt
¼ cup (60 mL) maple syrup
¼ cup (60 mL) coconut milk

Coconut Banana Cake

SERVES 6 TO 8

This started out as a version of a tres leches cake but evolved into entirely its own thing. Kathleen, the book's photographer, suggested more rum in the syrup (I'll leave it up to you to decide that), and that turned into a discussion about how nice banana would be on the side. Thus was created this cake—toasty and rummy with a light crumb and some moist banana chunks.

{ DAIRY-FREE · GLUTEN-FREE }

FOR THE CAKE

4 eggs, lightly beaten

¾ cup (175 mL) coconut milk

½ cup (125 mL) coconut sugar

⅓ cup (75 mL) unsweetened shredded coconut

¼ cup (60 mL) white sugar

½ tsp (2 mL) sea salt

1 cup (250 mL) brown rice flour

2 tsp (10 mL) baking powder

1 banana, cut in ½-inch (1 cm) slices

FOR THE SYRUP

1½ cups (375 mL) coconut milk

3 Tbsp (45 mL) coconut sugar

2 Tbsp (30 mL) rum of your choice

¾ cup (175 mL) unsweetened flaked coconut

1. Preheat oven to 350°F (180°C). Grease an 8-inch (20 cm) square cake pan with coconut oil and line with a 12- × 8-inch (30 × 20 cm) strip of parchment paper, leaving two "handles" to lift the baked cake out of the pan.

2. **MAKE THE CAKE** In a large bowl, combine eggs, coconut milk, coconut sugar, coconut, white sugar, and salt. Stir until well mixed. Add brown rice flour and baking powder; stir until batter is smooth. Stir in banana.

3. Pour batter into prepared pan and bake until a toothpick inserted in the middle of the cake comes out clean, 30 to 35 minutes.

4. **MEANWHILE, MAKE THE SYRUP** In a small saucepan over medium heat, cook coconut milk, coconut sugar, and rum, stirring often, until sugar is melted. Remove from heat and stir in coconut.

5. Remove cake from oven and preheat broiler. Let cool for about 10 minutes, then prick all over with a wooden skewer. Pour syrup evenly over cake. Let sit for about 2 minutes so cake can absorb liquid.

6. Holding parchment paper, lift cake out of pan and put it on a baking sheet. Broil on middle rack until edges and coconut are browned. Serve warm.

Almond Apple Cake

SERVES 6

This cake has a dense, moist texture and is fragrant with the promise of marzipan. Grind fresh almonds for the best almond flavor. I use ones with the skins on, as they are much healthier that way and the skins don't change the texture of the cake. This cake is best made the day before and wrapped tightly in plastic wrap until it is served. If you like, put it in a low oven to get it barely warm before serving alongside something creamy of your choice.

······{ DAIRY-FREE * GLUTEN-FREE }······

1. Preheat oven to 350°F (180°C). Grease an 8-inch (2 L) springform pan with coconut oil and line bottom with a circle of parchment paper.

2. In a food processor, combine almonds, coconut sugar, and salt. Blitz until almonds are very finely ground, about 30 seconds. Add brown rice flour, cornstarch, and baking powder; pulse until they are mixed through.

3. Add eggs and almond extract; process until a thick batter forms. Pour in coconut oil and process until batter is well combined, about 20 seconds.

4. Scrape batter into prepared pan. Arrange apple slices over top. Sprinkle evenly with sliced almonds, then with white sugar.

5. Bake until a toothpick inserted in the center of cake comes out clean, 45 to 50 minutes. Let cool in pan for about 20 minutes before serving. Run a knife around edge of cake before removing sides.

1⅓ cups (325 mL) whole almonds
¾ cup (175 mL) coconut sugar
½ tsp (2 mL) sea salt
2 Tbsp (30 mL) brown rice flour
2 Tbsp (30 mL) cornstarch
1 tsp (5 mL) baking powder
3 eggs
2 tsp (10 mL) almond extract
½ cup (125 mL) coconut oil, melted
1 Red Delicious apple, peeled, cored, and thinly sliced
½ cup (125 mL) sliced almonds
2 Tbsp (30 mL) white sugar

Drinks and Frozen Treats

RECIPES

Chai Tea Concentrate

MAKES ENOUGH CONCENTRATE FOR 6 TO 8 CUPS OF TEA

Keep this drink concentrate in a jar in your fridge for when the need
for a soothing cup of chai tea strikes—as it can at any time.

{ DAIRY-FREE * GLUTEN-FREE * VEGAN }

1. In a medium saucepan, combine tea bags, coconut sugar, peppercorns, fennel seeds, cardamom, cinnamon sticks, ginger, and water. Bring to a boil, reduce heat, and simmer for 5 minutes.

2. Remove from heat and let sit for at least 20 minutes.

3. Strain into a jar. Concentrate keeps, refrigerated, for a week.

- 8 tea bags (black, white, or green)
- 3 Tbsp (45 mL) coconut sugar
- 2 tsp (10 mL) black peppercorns
- 2 tsp (10 mL) fennel seeds
- 2 tsp (10 mL) cardamom pods, lightly crushed
- 2 cinnamon sticks
- 2 thumb-sized pieces fresh ginger, sliced ¼ inch (5 mm) thick
- 4 cups (1 L) water

FOR 1 CUP OF TEA

1. Combine chai concentrate and water; bring to a boil. Stir in coconut milk.

2. Pour into a mug and add sweetener to taste.

- ½ cup (125 mL) chai tea concentrate
- ¼ cup (60 mL) hot water
- ½ cup (125 mL) light coconut milk

Creamy Margarita

A cross between the classic margarita and an adult version of a Creamsicle. Enough said!

···················· { DAIRY-FREE * GLUTEN-FREE * VEGAN } ····················

1½ oz (45 mL) white tequila

1 oz (30 mL) coconut milk

1 Tbsp (15 mL) Cointreau

1 Tbsp (15 mL) lime juice

1 Tbsp (15 mL) agave syrup

A dash of bitters

1. Combine tequila, coconut milk, Cointreau, lime juice, agave syrup, and bitters in a cocktail shaker two-thirds full of ice cubes. Shake for about 20 seconds.

2. Pour over ice in a cocktail glass.

Spicy Pineapple Drink

There is a craze for spice in drinks, and I am a fan of this craze. Everyone we've served this to has loved it. You'll learn, after you make it once or twice, just how big your piece of red chili should be to make it spicy but not overwhelming.

{ DAIRY-FREE * VEGAN }

1. Combine coconut water, whiskey, pineapple juice, lime juice, chili, and agave syrup in a cocktail shaker two-thirds full of ice cubes. Shake vigorously for about 20 seconds.

2. Pour over ice in an Old-Fashioned glass.

2 oz (60 mL) unsweetened coconut water

1 oz (30 mL) spiced whiskey

1 oz (30 mL) pineapple juice

1 tsp (5 mL) lime juice

1-inch (2.5 cm) piece red chili, or to taste

A dash of agave syrup, or to taste

Greyhound

This drink is a classic. Using coconut water makes it even more refreshing than the original and smooths out the sour bite of the grapefruit juice.

························{ DAIRY-FREE ∗ GLUTEN-FREE ∗ VEGAN }························

2 oz (60 mL) grapefruit juice

1½ oz (45 mL) vodka

1 oz (30 mL) unsweetened coconut water

½ tsp (2 mL) lime juice

1. Combine grapefruit juice, vodka, coconut water, and lime juice in a cocktail shaker two-thirds full of ice cubes. Shake for about 20 seconds.

2. Pour over ice in an Old-Fashioned glass.

Egg-Free Eggnog

A delicious vegan version. The addition of salt may seem strange,
but it takes the nog from ho-hum to ho, ho, ho!

·······················{ DAIRY-FREE * GLUTEN-FREE * VEGAN }····················

1. In a medium jar, stir together coconut milk, rum, whiskey, maple syrup, water, vanilla, cinnamon, nutmeg, and salt. Mixture keeps, refrigerated, for up to 2 days.

2. For each drink, pour ⅓ cup (75 mL) mixture into a cocktail shaker two-thirds full of ice cubes. Shake for about 20 seconds. Pour over lots of ice in an Old-Fashioned glass. Garnish with a sprinkle of cinnamon and nutmeg, if desired.

1 cup (250 mL) coconut milk

4 oz (125 mL) dark rum

2 oz (60 mL) spiced whiskey

2 Tbsp (30 mL) maple syrup

2 Tbsp (30 mL) water

1 tsp (5 mL) vanilla extract

⅛ tsp (0.5 mL) cinnamon

⅛ tsp (0.5 mL) nutmeg

⅛ tsp (0.5 mL) sea salt

Watermelon Mint Pops

MAKES ABOUT 6 (½-CUP/125 ML) POPS

These pops are so refreshing. Taste and adjust the sweetness before
you freeze them, as freezing will make them taste less sweet.
Leave out the mint leaves if your kids don't like green stuff.

· { DAIRY-FREE * GLUTEN-FREE * VEGAN } ·

2 cups (500 mL) cubed
   watermelon, seeds removed

½ cup (125 mL) unsweetened
   coconut water

Juice of 1 lime

1 tsp (5 mL) agave syrup

⅛ tsp (0.5 mL) sea salt

A handful of small fresh
   mint leaves

1. In a blender, combine watermelon, coconut water, lime juice, agave syrup, and salt. Blend until smooth.

2. Place a few mint leaves in each popsicle mold. Divide watermelon mixture among molds. Freeze until firm, about 3 hours.

Fruit Cocktail Pops

MAKES ABOUT 6 (½-CUP/125 ML) POPS

These pops are gorgeous and a great way to use up all those ripening
fruits on your counter or in your fridge—and to get kids to eat their fruit.
Use any combination of fruit that you have on hand, such as grapes,
kiwifruit, strawberries, mango, pineapple, and banana.

·······················{·DAIRY-FREE * GLUTEN-FREE * VEGAN ·}························

1. In a medium bowl, combine fruit, mango nectar, coconut
   water, and agave syrup (if using). Stir until well mixed.

2. Divide among popsicle molds. Freeze until firm, about
   3 hours.

2 cups (500 mL) chopped fruit

½ cup (125 mL) mango nectar

½ cup (125 mL) unsweetened
coconut water

1 tsp (5 mL) agave syrup
(optional)

Blackberry and Coconut Pops

These pops are rich—more of a treat than a means of hydrating. Blackberries aren't for all kids, so go ahead and change up the fruit. The refrigeration step is important, as the colder the mixture is when you freeze it, the less likely it is to form crystals. And don't leave out the salt—it brightens the flavors of the coconut milk and berries and brings out their sweetness.

{ DAIRY-FREE * GLUTEN-FREE * VEGAN }

1 can (14 oz/400 mL) coconut milk

¼ cup (60 mL) agave syrup

⅛ tsp (0.5 mL) sea salt

Zest of ½ lemon

⅓ cup (75 mL) blackberries, raspberries, or blueberries

1. In a large bowl, stir together coconut milk, agave syrup, salt, and lemon zest until well mixed. Stir in blackberries. Refrigerate for at least 1 hour.

2. Divide among popsicle molds. Freeze until firm, about 4 hours.

Iced Coffee

MAKES ABOUT 4 CUPS (1 L)

Iced coffee is a refreshing way to get your caffeine on a hot day.
This version is quick to make. You don't even need to boil a kettle.
Remember to make the coconut water ice cubes ahead of time.

·····························{ DAIRY-FREE * GLUTEN-FREE * VEGAN }·····························

1. In a large pitcher, stir together hot water, espresso powder, and coconut sugar until espresso powder and sugar are dissolved.

2. Stir in coconut water and coconut milk. Serve over plenty of coconut water ice cubes.

¼ cup (60 mL) very hot water

2 Tbsp (30 mL) instant espresso powder

1 Tbsp (15 mL) coconut sugar

2½ cups (625 mL) cold unsweetened coconut water

1 cup (250 mL) cold light coconut milk

About 1½ cups (375 mL) unsweetened coconut water, frozen in an ice-cube tray

Acknowledgments

I'd like to thank:

My parents, Harry and Lil, for their encouragement and support throughout my very winding career path. I'd like to thank them also for tasting a lot of "coconut food," as we call it, and for their always honest feedback.

Jeanette, for grocery shopping and typing and tasting; Yotam, for his enthusiastic tasting of sometimes ten recipes in a day, and for keeping the kitchen in order; Beatrix, for making us laugh; and Cleo, for eating the stuff that fell on the floor—The Team.

Kathleen, for her beautiful photographs, quick work, great attitude, and bottomless appetite, and her husband, Dave, for holding down "le fort" in Paris.

Chefs Lynn and Lora, for showing me how it's done.

Shaun Oakey, for his patience and sense of humor throughout the editing process.

And Andrea Magyar, whose idea this was, for her support and always cheerful, candid, and quick replies to the many questions of a first-time cookbook author—The Boss.

Index